"Olivia Mellan's unique gift is her focus on the underlying issues involved in money conflicts so that real resolution and harmony are attainable for individuals, couples, and families."

—Harriet Lerner, Ph.D.,
author of *The Dance of Anger*

"In marriage, money is not the root of all evil, but overspending is certainly a prime source of conflict or anger. Ms. Mellan's book goes a long way toward alleviating this friction. After reading it, couples may achieve a better balance in their love life and their bank account."

—Bonnie Maslin, Ph.D.,
author of *The Angry Marriage*

"Practical suggestions for curbing self-destructive behavior. The book is never preachy and is enormously useful."

—*Publishers Weekly*

"An excellent book that should be read by all couples whether they think they have a problem with overspending or not."

—*Library Journal*

"A sympathetic program to help overspenders keep their habits under control and develop healthy attitudes toward money. The book is geared toward couples, but will help anyone who recognizes overspending as a problem."

—*Chicago Life*

"Covers a lot of new ground. . . . *Overcoming Overspending* doesn't purport to be a quick and easy guide to financial solvency. What it can do is help money-distressed couples get back on the right path together and preserve their most precious asset: each other."

—*San Diego Daily Transcript*

[handwritten inscription]

OVERCOMING
OVERSPENDING

A Winning Plan for Spenders and Their Partners

[handwritten inscription: With care & affection, Devin (Olivia) Mellan (Sheppard)]

OLIVIA MELLAN
with
SHERRY CHRISTIE

WALKER AND COMPANY
NEW YORK

Copyright © 1995 by Olivia Mellan

All rights reserved. No part of this book may be reproduced or transmitted in any form or by any means, electronic or mechanical, including photocopying, recording, or by any information storage and retrieval system, without permission in writing from the Publisher.

First published in the United States of America in 1995 by Walker Publishing Company, Inc.; first paperback edition published in 1997.

Published simultaneously in Canada by Thomas Allen & Son Canada, Limited, Markham, Ontario

Library of Congress Cataloging-in-Publication Data
Mellan, Olivia.
Overcoming overspending: a winning plan for spenders and their partners / Olivia Mellan with Sherry Christie.
p.   cm.
Published simultaneously in Canada by Thomas Allen.
Includes bibliographical references (p.   ).
ISBN 0-8027-1309-2
1. Compulsive shopping.   2. Compulsive shopping—Treatment.
3. Finance, Personal.   I. Christie, Sherry.   II. Title.
RC569.5.S56M45   1995
616.85′84—dc20   95-30128
CIP
_____
ISBN 0-8027-7495-4 (pbk.)

Book design by Claire Naylon Vaccaro

Printed in the United States of America

4   6   8   10   9   7   5   3

*To my husband, Michael, the best money mentor I could have
. . . who lives a life of money harmony and helps me evolve
toward one.*

Contents

PART THREE

Tools and Techniques You Both Can Use

PART FOUR

How Overspenders Can Overcome

Acknowledgments

I feel grateful to many who have made writing this book pleasurable and satisfying for me:

At Walker and Company, George Gibson was a delight and inspiration to me; he is a true friend and source of support in all ways. Jackie Johnson helped me clarify my vision; Judi Powers Kloos is a great publicist and a new, good friend. Barbara Monteiro is the reason I came to Walker in the first place; she still helps me in numerous business aspects of my career. In general, I appreciate Walker's integrity and willingness to involve me in all aspects of the publication process.

To all the clients who have deepened my appreciation of the complexity of the journey around overspending and related issues and who have pushed me forward in my own process as well: Thanks for being willing to share your journey with others so that they might learn enough to begin to heal and make new, more fulfilling choices around money and life goals.

To other money therapists, workshop leaders, and consultants in the field of money psychology: Arlene Modica Matthews, Victoria Felton Collins, Christopher Mogil and Anne Slepian, J. Grady Cash, Judy Barber, and others who continue to do such valuable work in getting the message out. And a special appreciation to Vicki Robin, whose work with Joe Dominguez and the New Road Map Foundation is making a powerful effort to transform our whole way of being with money and overconsumption.

To my financial planner friends, Peg Downey and Dick Vodra,

who provide me with important information, good advice, invaluable support, and warm friendship. To all the money professionals who have believed in me and felt I had much to offer to their field, thank you for your confidence and your enthusiasm.

To my close personal friends, Nancy Dunn, Carolyn Roth, Ira Chaleff, April Moore and Andy Schmookler, my brother Stu and his wife, Nancy, my dad, and the members of my women's and couples groups, for giving me the good advice and personal support necessary to persevere with a process that I find so challenging.

To my husband, Michael, who was a solid model of sanity, balance, and nonjudgmental good advice in the area of money management and wise use of money. To my son Aniel, whose honesty in discussions with me always teaches me something. To Anne Anderson, who made my first writing possible and continues to serve as a sounding board and friend when I am in need. To all the folks at the Washington Therapy Guild, my original professional "family." To Louise Klok, who helps me do the deepest work on myself so I can try to "walk my talk."

And finally, my thanks to Sherry Christie, for her brilliant writing and for her ability to tune in to the intent of my words, to translate my message so much better than I could have done on my own.

Introduction

Overspending: The Billion-Dollar Addiction Hiding in Closets All Over the Country

As a therapist specializing in money conflicts, I've worked for over twenty years with individuals and couples who struggle daily to overcome one of today's most widespread problems: overspending.

Many of us wonder at times whether we spend too much. But to characterize yourself or a loved one as an *over*spender may seem a bit . . . extreme. Okay, so maybe you do go through a juggling act worthy of the Flying Karamazov Brothers to pay each month's bills—but that would undoubtedly improve if you had more money. Though, come to think of it, your last raise didn't seem to make much difference. And your nearest and dearest, who used to joke that money burns a hole in your pocket, isn't laughing about it anymore.

In assessing our spending habits, we're also apt to insist that we have good reasons for being a little extravagant—reasons that make sense to us, anyway. For example, spending may be a way to feel close to our loved ones as we splurge on gifts for birthdays, holidays, and other occasions, even though these bills put us in debt for months. Or spending may help us fulfill an internal (and perhaps unconscious) image of ourselves. Three far-from-unusual self-images of this kind are the Trend Surfer, who insists on being the first to buy and show off every new electronic gizmo; the Tasteful Sophisticate, who shops constantly for elegant and exotic knickknacks to create the home beautiful; and the Daredevil, who craves the high-stakes thrill of gambling or high-risk investing.

What determines whether this behavior is harmless—mere generosity, pleasure in one's possessions, or the joy of pitting oneself against the odds—or the problem conduct of a shopaholic, riskaholic, or overspender?

There are specific attitudes toward money that characterize overspenders, but the basic definition is this: If your spending habits create a problem for you or others around you, you're probably an overspender. It's as simple (and as complex) as that.

A Society of Overstressed Overspenders

If you're an overspender or in a relationship with one, you've experienced some of the financial and emotional stresses this behavior can cause: excessive debt, credit problems, distrust, anger, hurt, guilt, slumping self-esteem. The solution isn't to earn more money; this just adds fuel to an out-of-control fire. Without a positive strategy for healing, matters can become even worse as frustrated overspenders seek escape in their habitual consolation: more spending.

Part of the problem is that we live in a culture where family fragmentation, household mobility, and employment insecurity combine to make many of us feel lonely and alienated, disconnected from community, and at a loss for ways to give form and meaning to our lives. These feelings of emptiness intensify the urge to fill ourselves up with "things"—the self-gratifying services and self-defining status symbols that money buys.

Such rewards are also the way many of us have conditioned ourselves to cope with everyday pressures. Was the boss a real pain in the neck today? Kids acting up? Reeling from a fender bender on the freeway or an IRS audit notice in the mail? *Poor baby*, we say to ourselves, *go buy yourself a special treat. You deserve it!*

When things aren't going too well in an intimate relationship, these feelings of alienation and stress can compound each other. To make up for a lack of warmth or fulfillment at home, it's not unusual for one partner (or both) to fill the void by rushing out with a credit card and buying something.

In my therapy practice, I've seen how out-of-control buying affects not only overspenders themselves but the people in close relationships with them—spouses or significant others, business partners, parents, or adult children.

Overspending takes its toll in fractured relationships and broken families, along with increased caseloads at Consumer Credit Counseling Service offices and bankruptcy courts. It's more than just a societal trend. I believe it's a societal addiction.

Overspenders will find there are a number of books available with advice on how to get out of debt and/or change behavior. But compulsive spending is far from easy to resolve. It takes tremendous vigilance, fortitude, and courage

A Self-Help Handbook for Overspenders—and Those Who Care About Them

—and a great deal of outside support so the journey does not feel too overwhelming.

In fact, it's very difficult for an overspender in a relationship to recover without the help of his or her partner. But up until now, very little has been written to help these relationship partners understand the inner world of someone struggling to curb the impulse to spend money, or to show them how they can make the recovery process easier.

That's why this book is addressed not just to overspenders, but also to those who care about them. In it, both of you can learn how to confront and heal the causes of overspending and to guide your mutual relationship toward what I call money harmony—a state of balance where you feel free to save, spend, or invest your money in a way that reflects your deeper values, goals, and integrity.

| How to Get the Most Out of This Guide | In the table of contents, you'll see that *Overcoming Overspending* is divided into sections, some of them directed to both of you, and others aimed specifically at the spender or the spender's partner. |

If you're an overspender who isn't in a partner relationship, the chapters that are oriented toward partners can still be helpful to you. They can help you cultivate the proper attitude of loving, detached self-acceptance, and patience. Alternatively, you may want to share the book with other people in your life who can help you heal.

In any case, spenders should feel free to read chapters in the order that feels most valuable to their own path of healing.

On a personal level, I know success is possible—because I myself am a recovering overspender. The help of my supportive and nonjudgmental spouse has been an enormously important factor in my recovery. I've benefited, too, from the opportunity to guide and support others working toward money harmony in my therapy sessions, workshops, interviews, and public speaking.

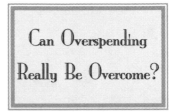

Can Overspending Really Be Overcome?

One of my basic therapy principles is that recovery can only be built on your strengths, not on your weaknesses. In your dialogues (internal or with your partner), there's no point in dwelling on such themes as "If only I hadn't been so extravagant, all our debts would have been paid by now" or "How could I/you go out and buy that new outfit when there are so many more important things we need?" People don't change when they are made to feel bad about themselves. Only by first acknowledging their strong points—areas of their life where they feel okay or even gifted—are people empowered to confront and overcome their shortcomings.

You'll find compassion as well as concrete help in this book. I feel strongly that you should give yourself credit for having the courage to take these positive steps and should reward yourself for changing habits you've had for years. Don't blame yourself or your partner if progress is slow or if your resolution falters and you backslide temporarily. In overcoming overspending, you may be trying to give up a compulsion that's as powerful as cigarettes are to a smoker.

As you begin to work on overcoming overspending, you may feel as though you take a step back for every step forward. But if you're tenacious in following the therapy principles in this book, you'll find these backward steps eventually shrink to half a step, and then disappear, allowing you to move freely into a financial future where you feel more satisfied and whole.

❧

PART ONE

What Is Overspending

All About?

1.

Born to Shop

Sitting with her husband in my office, Rita was close to tears as she talked about their new truck.

A bank teller, she'd married Brian after an "incredibly romantic" courtship. They'd met at the customer service counter of the warehouse store where he was assistant manager. Brian had sent her roses every day until she agreed to go out with him; then he'd wined and dined her at the best restaurants in town. He finally arranged for a plane to skywrite MARRY ME RITA in the middle of an outdoor rock concert they were attending.

Now, Rita explained, they were ready to settle down and start saving to buy a home. At least, *she* was. But because Brian really enjoyed wining and dining, they continued to eat out three or four nights a week. And now those impulsive gifts that had once seemed so wonderful—a sweater he thought she'd like, an electronic pocket organizer for himself—were putting a lot of strain on their limited finances.

They'd talked about curbing their spending, but every month Rita went through the same nerve-racking struggle to pay the bills. When Brian announced he'd just traded in his old sedan for a new 4x4 pickup, she nearly panicked. Her immediate reaction was "You'll bankrupt us!"

Obviously unhappy that Rita didn't trust him to act responsibly, Brian protested. "Why should I beat myself up working fifty hours a week if it means waiting forever to enjoy my money? Besides, I'm in line for a promotion that will mean a bigger salary, and driving an old clunker is no way to impress my boss."

How to Identify an Overspending Problem

In the introduction to this book, I suggested that no matter what your reasons for openhanded spending may be, if this behavior causes problems for yourself or your relationships, you're probably an overspender. *Probably*—because it's possible your partner is such an overhoarder that *any* spending may seem excessive to him or her.

What finally identified Brian as an overspender were his responses to the following quiz, which I often use to help open people's eyes to the existence of a serious problem.

TAKE THIS SELF-DIAGNOSTIC
QUIZ FOR OVERSPENDERS

If you know you have an overspending problem, your first step should be to determine the issues you'll want to work on.

At this early stage of the discovery process, I suggest that both partners take the following quiz. You may find you're both spenders, one perhaps more extreme than the other. Whether this is the case, or one of you is a spender and the other a hoarder, it can be helpful to see just how far apart you are in your spending behavior.

Since a simple *yes* or *no* answer doesn't give you much latitude, I suggest you respond with *often* (*O*), *sometimes* (*S*), *rarely* (*R*), or *never* (*N*). The more accurate you can be, the better.

1. Do you buy things you want, whether or not you can afford them at the moment? *O   S   R   N*

2. Do you have trouble saving money? If you have a little extra available to put in the bank, do you tend to think of something you'd rather spend it on? *O   S   R   N*

3. Do you buy things to cheer yourself up or to reward yourself? *O   S   R   N*

4. Does more than a third of your income go to pay bills (not including mortgage or rent payments)? *O   S   R   N*

5. Do you juggle bill paying because you always seem to be living on the edge financially? For example, do you tend to pay only the minimum balance on your credit cards? *O   S   R   N*

6. Do you tend to keep buying more of your favorite things—clothes, CDs, books, computer software, electronic gadgets—even if you don't have a specific need for them? *O   S   R   N*

7. If you have to say *no* to yourself, or put off buying something you really want, do you feel intensely deprived, angry, or upset? *O   S   R   N*

HOW TO EVALUATE YOUR ANSWERS

If you have four or more *O*'s or *S*'s, you definitely have overspending tendencies. Heavy bills can result from a temporary emergency, of course. But if you're perpetually deep in debt and have trouble delaying gratification until you can afford what you want, you're an overspender. Give yourself credit for facing up to this answer— for honesty is the first step in recovery.

COMPARE YOUR ANSWERS WITH YOUR PARTNER'S

It can be illuminating for partners to compare their perceptions of their own behavior. Which answers to the quiz do the two of you agree on most closely? Where do your perceptions differ most widely?

For example, when Brian told Rita he'd answered "often" to the last question ("If you have to say *no* to yourself . . . do you feel intensely deprived, angry, or upset?"), she was taken aback. As a logical, controlled hoarder, she'd never been aware of the deep emotional frustration Brian felt when he had to deny himself something he wanted. Moments of insight like this can help each of you understand where the other one is coming from.

Typically, the dynamics of your relationship will fit one of five patterns. In any of these patterns, the two of you are likely to have different priorities, and often different values:

> ✶ One of you is at heart an overspender, the other a hoarder, drawn together like Juliet and Romeo.

- You're both spenders, one mild and the other more extreme.

- One partner's overspending has turned the other into a hoarder, compulsive about the need to save money and fearful of spending it on passing pleasures.

- One partner's extreme hoarding is prompting the other to overspend in rebellion against this stinginess and overcontrol.

- One partner's extreme hoarding is causing him or her to view the other's relatively moderate spending as excessive.

As you discuss your respective viewpoints in this exercise, the important thing isn't who's right or who's wrong, but where you feel you (and your partner) stand in regard to spending. Try to listen to each other's answers as empathetically as possible, looking for areas where you can agree. If you have a different opinion, voice it in a calm, nonconfrontational way. Hostile accusations can burn bridges, while caring communication helps build them.

For example, you might say, "I notice you feel we rarely juggle our bill paying. Would you be willing to sit down with me once a month so we can pay our bills together? I'd welcome your help, and it may give you a better idea of our situation." Or "It's interesting that you say you often buy things to cheer yourself up. I hadn't realized that. Is there something I could do (or not do) to help cheer you up in other ways?"

Why Can't an Overspender Just Snap Out of It?

Like an alcoholic trying to stay sober at a party with heavy drinkers, overspenders find their resolve to "just say no" continually challenged by their environment—a society where spending is the norm. Their friends and coworkers, not to mention popular culture in general, treat the issue of overspending with a kind of flippant humor that makes light of this serious addiction.

From Moosehead Lake to Malibu, T-shirts and tote bags trumpet "Shop till you drop," "Veni, Vidi, Visa[R]," "See Jane charge. Charge, Jane, charge," and "When the going gets tough, the tough go shopping." An occasional slogan may admit the absurdity of our spendaholism, like "The one who dies with the most toys wins." But by and large, we rarely acknowledge the sad truth that many of us still long for deep satisfaction and fulfillment despite our surfeit of material goods and comforts.

A THOROUGHLY MODERN MALADY

America wasn't always the land of blue-light specials and Barbie dolls.[1] In fact, we started the century with a rather austere ethic, partly Puritan and partly capitalist, that stressed moral qualities: hard work, honesty, sacrifice, character. Rewards came from contributing or producing. Like the generations before them, our great-grandparents were raised with the stern Biblical belief that "Whatsoever a man soweth, so shall he reap"—a theme reinforced by the moralistic messages of McGuffey's *Reader* and Horatio Alger's rags-to-riches tales of earnest, enterprising young heroes.

But in the 1920s and '30s, a new way of thinking began to emerge, nourished by a surge of breakthrough discoveries and inventions such as electricity, telephones, automobiles, household appliances, radio, television, movies, and air travel. These dazzling developments understandably caused a lot of excitement—after all, people had been relying on horse-drawn transportation and oil lamps for thousands of years.

One of the results was a wave of idealism. Many hoped this

scientific progress might produce solutions to fundamental human and social problems, opening up a new world of fulfillment and liberation. This optimism led to a variety of ambitious solutions such as Prohibition (to end the scourge of demon rum), women's suffrage (to extend voting rights to the remaining 50 percent of U.S. adults), communism (to destroy the oppression of despots), and the New Deal (to level the economic playing field for workers devastated by the Great Depression).

A second result of the breakthroughs was an unprecedented spate of new goods and services. Department stores and supermarkets sprang up, offering one-stop shopping, volume prices, and more choice than the neighborhood Mom-and-Pops. And to communicate all this abundance, America reinvented advertising.

Until this giddy period of the '20s and '30s, most ads were local and low-key, simply announcing the availability of a product or service to meet a need ("Eggs 5¢ a dozen," "Jacobs Furriers"). But now, the avalanche of novel concepts and unfamiliar new products meant advertising often had to persuade large numbers of people to buy things they'd never bought before and had never thought they might want.

After World War II, Madison Avenue really cranked into high gear. As retailing analyst Victor Lebow wrote at the time, "Our enormously productive economy . . . demands that we make consumption our way of life, that we convert the buying and use of goods into rituals, that we seek our spiritual satisfaction, our ego satisfaction, in consumption. . . . We need things consumed, burned up, worn out, replaced, and discarded at an ever-increasing rate."[2]

Everywhere people turned, they were reminded they were consumers. Billboards, newspaper and magazine ads, TV and radio commercials, store flyers, bus and subway cards, supermarket cart cards, blimp signs, sponsor IDs on everything from race cars to golf tournaments . . . marketing's reach became (and still is) infinite.

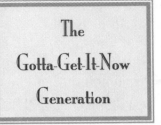

The Gotta-Get-It-Now Generation

After the deprivations of the Depression and World War II, the self-denial and hard work of the old sow-and-reap tradition paled in comparison with the glamour of the new consumer-centered culture. Our parents or grandparents gladly embraced the postwar delights of a new Maytag or a Levittown ranch with attached carport. However, they'd paid heavy dues to enjoy this bounty; we, their children, haven't. Born into the new culture, we take its material rewards for granted. Instead of McGuffey's moralizing and *Luck and Pluck*, we've absorbed our values from TV shows where any problem can be solved in sixty minutes or less, with the promise of personal health, wealth, and/or happiness thrown in as a bonus by the sponsor.

Today, we're bombarded from infancy with images of all the wonderful things we can buy to transform our lives into bliss and perfection. (By one estimate, American kids have seen an average of 360,000 ads by the time they graduate from high school.)[3] Once we decide to purchase something, ownership can be ours with a quick trip to a nearby store or market. We can order even more easily by phone from a catalog or TV shopping show—or simply point and click as we scan an electronic mall on the Internet.

In other words, we've created a culture that not only fosters overspending, but makes it almost impossible to kick the habit. Consider these statistics, rounded up from a variety of sources:

* A typical U.S. parent spends forty minutes a week playing with his or her children and six hours a week shopping, according to *The Wall Street Journal*.[4]

* 93 percent of American girls say store hopping is a "favorite activity," reports Laurence Shames in *The Hunger for More*.[5]

* Our favorite pastime is going to the mall and "waiting for the urge to buy something to hit us," as *Fire in the Belly* author Sam Keen puts it.[6]

* Impulse purchases account for about half of all sales at grocery and hardware stores. And in a recent survey reported by *The Wall Street Journal*, only one in four mall shoppers was looking for a particular item.[7]

* Shopping at home has become a $2.5 billion business. In the next five years, it's expected to burgeon to as much as $100 billion.[8]

It's important to understand the extraordinary power of the forces influencing us to overspend. Take enclosed shopping malls, for instance. As a recovering overspender, I find malls a particularly dangerous place to spend time. To me, their all-under-one-roof profusion of goodies encourages a trancelike state of euphoria overspenders can get into when they're on a binge. At least when the stores are geographically separated, you're forced to get a breath of fresh air before going from one to the next!

Overspenders will increasingly find their willpower under attack in the privacy of their own homes, as the scientific revolution takes another quantum leap with the spread of cable and satellite systems and the introduction of new interactive technologies. To maintain our emotional and economic health, we must learn not to cave in to subtle (and sometimes not-so-subtle) pressures to fill ourselves up with "things" and keep up with our free-spending peers.

Right now, many of us are having a tough time resisting the lure of easy credit. With credit card companies coaxing prospective applicants with "low introductory rates" and merchants promising "90 days same as cash," why not buy whatever you want? Why, it's almost as though you had the money in your pocket!

Unfortunately, what you probably have instead is debt. Lots of it.

- From 1990 to 1994, Americans took on 32.4 percent more household debt (totaling about $4.5 trillion), says economist Robert Eisner in *The Wall Street Journal.*[9] That's on top of increasing our debt load 162 percent during the course of the preceding decade, according to *Money* magazine![10]

- In 1991, the typical U.S. household was $8,750 in debt (not including mortgage), according to *Money.*"[11]

- In 1990, 83 percent of U.S. disposable income went to pay off debt; in 1983, the figure was only 62 percent.[12]

- Between 1973 and 1993, the percentage of disposable income allocated to savings plunged from 8.6 to 4.2 percent.[13]

- Spending increases an average of 23 percent when credit cards are used instead of cash, report David Wallechinsky and Irving Wallace in *The People's Almanac.*[14]

- The average American carries nine credit cards with a combined balance of about $1,600, up 23 percent since 1992.[15]

- In 1994, we charged $701 billion on credit cards, 25 percent more than in 1993.[16]

- The average amount of credit-card debt carried by consumers requesting help with debt reduction is $14,000, according to the Bankcard Holders of America, a national consumer organization.[17]

- More than 1 million consumers called Consumer Credit Counseling Service offices for help in 1993—a 25-percent increase over 1992.[18]

* 1992 bankruptcy filings reached nearly one million—triple the number filed in 1981, *The New York Times* reports.[19]

* Debtors Anonymous, a free twelve-step program similar to Alcoholics Anonymous, is beginning new chapters all over the country in response to consumer need.

The saddest thing about this societal addiction to overspending is that our headlong pursuit of material things doesn't seem to be bringing us happiness.

To cite just one piece of evidence: when a group of 18- to 29-year-olds were surveyed back in 1978, more than 40 percent of them felt they had a very good chance of achieving the "good life." In a similar poll in 1993, that percentage nosedived to just 21 percent, according to *The Wall Street Journal*.[20] During this time, per-capita consumption in this country increased by something on the order of 45 percent.[21] What happened? What has made today's young people more pessimistic, when they should be pleased by their enhanced ability to buy what they want?

These and other observations indicate that we're beginning to realize that "more" is not necessarily "better," and that in spite of (or perhaps because of) our preoccupation with having more and more material comforts, conveniences, and pleasures, our real underlying needs are not being met.

STOP THE WHIRL—I WANT TO
GET OFF!

Earlier in this chapter, I mentioned that this century's early technological bloom also produced a sense of hope—a belief that these new tools might help us create a better, more fulfilling life free of disease, drudgery, and despair.

This hope survives, I think, deep inside all of us. It's the reason why material things don't satisfy us. Our abundance and our aspirations are twins, born of the same explosion of creative energy. One day, I hope, we as a society will be able to find the way these two gifts are meant to be combined, the right balance, the harmony we're meant to achieve.

At present, this utopia seems as far away as Uranus to millions of American consumers. Perhaps overspending is a phase our culture must mature out of. Like kids who've been handed the keys to the candy store, we may have to experience the discomfort of overindulgence before we learn how to handle the abundance that surrounds us. It's heartening to imagine that recovering overspenders might be among the pioneers of this new era!

Until then, overspenders like Brian will face a daily barrage of enticement and seduction. Eroding their resistance even more are the attitudes toward money learned from their parents and other role models, a subject we'll explore in the next chapter.

As a therapist, I see a lot of value in examining the cultural pressures behind overspending, as we've done here. If you're in a relationship with an overspender, understanding societal pressures can help you view your partner's behavior and money attitudes with more compassion. And if you are an overspender yourself, this awareness can ease feelings of guilt and shame, and dispel the false notion that you're alone in your struggle against overspending.

You were not born to shop. You were born to be free and in harmony with the world around you. By understanding the societal forces pulling on you like a dark moon, you'll take the first step toward freedom.

2.

Why Do We Overspend?

As I began working with Brian and Rita, the couple described in chapter 1, they responded in strikingly different ways to our discussion of societal pressures to overspend. At her bank, Rita often witnessed the results of overspending: customers who repeatedly made only the minimum monthly payment on their credit cards or home equity lines; other customers who called regularly, annoyed and upset, when they received a checking-account overdraft notice.

"I've seen as much advertising as anyone, but I've never bounced a check—and I never will!" Rita insisted vehemently. "People who live on the edge like that are irresponsible. Before I buy anything, I always check to make sure I can afford to spend the money."

Catching herself speaking as if she were still single, she shot a half-embarrassed, half-defiant look at Brian, as if to say, *And that's the way you'd be, if you were as sensible as I am!*

Brian, who spent every working day in a spending environment at the warehouse store, had seemed relieved to find his own impulses validated by the pressures we'd talked about. Now he retorted, "Rita, you sound like an old skinflint! If I see something I want for myself or think you'd enjoy having, I need to feel free to buy it!"

How can we explain such opposite attitudes toward money? There's clearly more to our behavior than just the culture surrounding us. Otherwise, we'd *all* be spenders, instead of falling into a number of different "money types" I've identified in my therapy work.[1]

The three types most often involved in overspending relationships are spenders, hoarders, and bingers.

> *Spenders*, as we've seen, love to use their money to buy whatever will bring them pleasure, including gifts for others. They may have a hard time budgeting, saving, and postponing gratification to meet a long-term goal. Overspenders have extreme spender tendencies. They often spend all the money they have and then some, plunging themselves into ever-deepening indebtedness. (As we've noted before, debt alone does not a spender make. If you have trouble paying for life's necessities, your income simply may not be adequate.)

> *Hoarders*, the polar opposite of spenders, enjoy holding onto money. They're often excellent at saving and budgeting, but find it difficult to spend money on nonessential purchases for themselves or their loved ones. As I mentioned earlier, if one partner in a relationship has strong spender tendencies, the other partner often develops into a hoarder to restore financial balance, even if he or she wasn't a hoarder to begin with. By the same token, someone in a relationship with a committed hoarder can develop into a spender, out of frustration at being forced to give up or postpone the pleasures that money can buy.

✻ *Bingers* are part spender and part hoarder—an unstable combination. They tend to save and save, appearing quite controlled and focused, until something triggers them into a wild spending binge. During this out-of-control episode, they'll blow some or all of the money they've so carefully saved. Unfortunately, bingers usually can't predict when the next urge to splurge will strike, possibly plunging them into serious overspending and debt.

Many people in spender relationships may also incorporate aspects of other money types in their attitudes toward spending.

✻ *Amassers* believe that greater wealth means greater power, status, or self-worth. Thus, they tend to put a lot of time and effort into managing their money—spending hours hunting for the best CD rate, shifting investments every time the stock market hiccups, and endlessly manipulating the data in their personal-finance computer programs. Some amassers may spend lavishly to impress others and flaunt their wealth. By contrast, an amasser who enters a relationship with a spender may begin behaving like a hoarder to prevent the spender from depleting their painstakingly stockpiled money. Carried to extremes, this obsession can come to dominate their lives, preventing them from enjoying the fruits of their labor in a fun, spontaneous way.

✻ *Worriers* have big-time anxiety about their finances. They feel it's their responsibility to try to control their money, so in addition to spending hours checking on their account balances, they also expend a lot of emotional energy imagining and worrying about other things that could happen to it. Like other kinds of money behavior, worrying is a deeply rooted attitude. Thus, although worriers often believe they'd stop worrying if they had more money, the truth is that they'd just have more to worry about. Most hoarders are worriers. In a relationship with an overspender, they tend to become more extreme in both their hoarding and their worrying.

❦ Avoiders tend to ignore, postpone, or delegate the tasks of everyday money management. They may feel nervous about taking on the responsibility of handling their own money and fearful of making mistakes. (Though women tend to feel less confident about money decisions than men do, avoiders can be of either gender.) Most spenders are also avoiders.

❦ Money monks fear that accumulated wealth or a habit of ostentatious spending may come to control them, limiting their freedom. Uneasy if they have a lot of money, they often live frugally, following the credo of "When you got nothin', you got nothin' to lose." Because of their distrust of money, money monks often don't have much sympathy with other money types. An extreme spender in a relationship with a money monk will face a lot of conflict unless they both can move to more moderate positions. If not, they'd probably do better with separate bank accounts.

Where do these attitudes come from? What gives people like Brian the tendency to become spenders in the first place . . . and predisposes people in relationships with them, like Rita, to become hoarders? More often than not, the answer lies in our past.

As the Twig Is Bent . . .

As very young children, we have no conception of what money is or isn't. While we're growing up, our attitudes toward money are formed by what we learn from our parents, relatives, religious instructors, and other role models, as well as by messages from our peers and from society in general.

Unfortunately, this important subject is seldom discussed calmly and rationally in families. In fact, I call money "the last taboo," since most parents are a lot more willing to level with their kids about sex and drugs than to talk about sensible behavior toward money. Thus, children are left to pick up information and attitudes from the example of their elders.

As a result, the money behavior we exhibit as adults often has its roots in habits we witnessed in our childhood. As you may already know if you've read my first book, *Money Harmony*, most of us tend either to mirror the behavior of our parents or other influences, or to act in a way that's the polar opposite of theirs. For example, if your mother was constantly anxious about money, her behavior could influence you to grow up into a worrier, too. Or seeing her compulsion to scrimp and sacrifice, you may vow never to let your adult self feel so deprived . . . and grow up a spender instead.

To explore the reasons behind the money conflict in Rita's and Brian's relationship, I invited both of them to share their recollections of how money was handled in their families.

Rita's money memories centered on her father, a senior official in the small bank that served their farming community. From as far back as she could remember, she'd heard her dad preach the danger of becoming financially overextended and predict disaster for farmers who took on unmanageable debt to buy expensive equipment. She vividly remembered attending a bankruptcy auction with her parents when she was just eight or nine, and watching a schoolmate break down in tears as his home and farm animals were sold.

As Rita told this story, which clearly still had the power to upset her, I could see Brian beginning to make the connections between those long-ago lessons and his wife's present behavior. He was thoughtful and subdued as he told us about his own military family, where, as far as he could remember, money had not been an issue. His mother had managed the household finances, since his dad was frequently gone on special duty.

Suddenly his face brightened with a pleasant memory. "He'd always bring home something for us from wherever he'd been. Once he got me a Cornhuskers sweatshirt when he was in Nebraska. Man, I wore that sweatshirt till it was in shreds. It made me feel good, like Dad was home with us."

This cherished memory helped reveal the roots of Brian's impulse spending. In bringing home gifts for himself, he was reassuring himself he was okay, loved, and safe, as his often-absent father had told him by bringing him presents so many years earlier. When he bought gifts for Rita, he was mirroring the way his dad had expressed love and affection for his own family.

It's not unusual for spenders to believe that money equals love or that spending can make up for a lack of love. In fact, spendthrift behavior often has its roots in early feelings of deprivation. Starved of the emotional, physical, or material nourishment we need, we resolve (often unconsciously) to provide it for ourselves when we grow up. But as adults, we are exposed to a culture that says consumption is the pathway to love, happiness, and fulfillment. We'll be the envy of our friends and attract hordes of prospective mates, we're told, simply by buying this sporty car, that big-screen TV, or the right designer clothes.

By emulating his father's spending behavior, Brian was reassuring himself that he was still lovable and showing Rita that he loved her. Fortunately, thanks to his basically happy childhood and his feelings of fulfillment in his relationship with Rita, he hadn't become an extreme overspender. His understanding of Rita's dad's stern warnings about indebtedness—and especially her vivid childhood memory of the farm auction—helped him to appreciate why she was so worried about his spending. In turn, Brian's openness allowed Rita to understand and empathize with his feelings about spending, in spite of her hoarder upbringing.

After working together on therapy exercises that helped each of them move toward the middle, this young couple was eventually able to develop a spending plan they could both feel comfortable with.

Deep inside, most overspenders believe money can buy, or substitute for, love or happiness. It's also not unusual to find spending and/or amassing money equated with power (a concept held more often by men than by women).

"Can't Buy Me Love" . . . or Can It?

All these beliefs have one thing in common: they're myths. For example, it may feel good to show your affection with a costly gift. But your loved one may appreciate and cherish far more such expressions of love as hugs, kisses, heartfelt compliments, or an offer to wash the dishes after dinner.

By the same token, when you buy things for yourself to compensate for a feeling of emptiness and lack of love, it's like feeding yourself empty calories. You may feel gratified by the appearance, the aroma, the taste—the whole sensory experience of consuming—but shortly afterward you feel hungry again, because you haven't really been nourished. Unless you change your attitudes and your behavior, this emotional malnutrition can lead to low self-esteem and other psychological problems.

(This analogy with overeating is more than just a metaphor. Clinicians suspect that overspending, overeating, and other "consuming" compulsions may have similar roots, since some over-

spenders who forcibly choke off their spending tend to find themselves overeating or smoking instead.[2] To develop tools and tactics
that overspenders, overeaters, and smokers can use to free themselves, we must get to the root of these behaviors.)

Compulsive spending can be a problem for several kinds of
personalities. Do you recognize yourself among any of these?

- *The "Money Is Love" Spender.* Motive: to show affection to self or
others or to relieve guilt. May buy on impulse, often triggered by stress.

- *The Blue-Light Spender.* Motive: bargain hunting. Buys items on
sale, almost always without comparison shopping.

- *The Esteem Spender.* Motive: peer approval. Buys top brand
names and prestigious labels from exclusive stores. Wouldn't be
caught dead in Wal-Mart.

- *The Overboard Spender.* Motive: insatiable need—a habit or addiction, hobby, or collection. Buying is often excessive by normal
standards and may be uncontrollable.

- *The "I'll Show You" Spender.* Motive: get revenge, show power, or
feel superior to someone.

- *The Spin-of-the-Wheel Spender.* Motive: thrill of testing oneself
against the fates (e.g., the stock market or the roulette wheel). Enjoys
the intensity of feeling at risk.[3]

Are You a Compulsive Spender?

Like many overspenders, you may be a combination of two or more of the personalities just described. For example, "Money Is Love" spenders are often Overboard spenders too. No matter what your personality type, you are a compulsive spender if you fit this profile:

* You tend to spend money when you go shopping, whether or not you need anything.

* You often buy things or take financial risks regardless of whether you can really afford them.

* When life gets too stressful, you seek consolation by spending or risking money.

* When you feel lonely, anxious, depressed, or bored, you spend to cheer yourself up.

* Your favorite way of celebrating or rewarding yourself is to spend or gamble a lot of money.

Overspending can also be a way of numbing ourselves to past or present fears, anxieties, or injuries. Like eating, spending is often the solace we learn to seek when we're feeling lonely, sad, frightened, helpless, unfulfilled, or unlovable. Maybe it's not really love or happiness, we may admit to ourselves, but it's better than nothing.

That's why we resist giving up these habits so strongly, no matter how unhappy we may be with their long-term effect. It's scary out there. *Gee*, the child in us whispers, *I don't want to be all alone!* Without this defense against the world, maybe we won't be okay, maybe we won't be safe.

For this reason, it's rare for an overspender—whether a blue-light buyer or an "I'll Show You" shopper—to be able to quit cold turkey. Even if the spender promises solemnly to keep to a budget and never splurge again, another binge will inevitably occur and the cycle will begin anew unless the causes of his or her behavior are addressed. To heal, we must learn to find our solace in more nourishing kinds of behavior—a process we'll explore in detail in the next chapters.

What Gender Is an Overspender?

There used to be a stereotype that women were spenders and men were hoarders. If that was ever true, and I have my doubts, it certainly isn't any longer. It's fair to say, however, that men and women tend to overspend on different things. Men are more likely to buy high-tech items like sophisticated cars, electronic equipment, and watches, or indulge in high-risk activities like gambling and exotic investments. Women, on the other hand, are more apt to buy clothes, cosmetics, and items to beautify or showcase the home.

When we look at how men and women are brought up and the cues they're given in advertising, these differences make sense. Men are encouraged to seek power symbols that will earn the admiration of their peers, while women are told to find ways of demonstrating their homemaking skills, beauty, or desirability. Generalizations like these don't fit everyone, of course, but in my experience they describe many male and female overspenders.

Men and women also have different defenses and vulnerabilities when they try to confront their destructive money behavior. Men, for example, often find it difficult to tolerate feeling incompetent or stupid. Because they see it as humiliating not to have their "moneylife" in order, they tend to cover up their weaknesses in this area. The loving partner of a male overspender must learn to discuss this difficulty in a sensitive and gentle way that doesn't make him feel put down or belittled.

By contrast, women tend to assume personal blame for their overspending. Quick to infer that their out-of-control behavior will cause them to be considered irresponsible, selfish, unloving, or a bad wife or mother, they may react with fear or defensiveness to their partner's attempt to address the subject. Instead of being angry or hostile and making matters worse, the partner of a female overspender needs to learn to discuss the subject in a caring, empathetic, nonjudgmental way.

Way up there, almost higher than you can see, your partner is piloting a fragile craft above an unknown landscape without chart or compass, buffeted by headwinds and thunderheads, on a nerve-racking journey toward peace, stability, and wholeness. To this lonely  traveler, you are the one whose company means the most, whose listening, questioning, encouraging, and caring can make it easier to navigate the unbeaconed wilderness.

In the next chapter, I'll tell you of my own painful journey—and how a caring partner helped to bring me home.

3.

"It Sweeps Over Me Like

a Tidal Wave"

What happens when an overspender or binger is caught up in the urge to buy? A typical overspending episode proceeds through five phases:

1. *Trigger.* This may be a one-time experience (good news or a stressful event) or accumulated feelings of anger, loneliness, rejection, helplessness, depression, anxiety, fear, and/or boredom.

2. *Consent.* Desire and decision merge as you quickly identify what you want and give yourself permission to get it.

3. *Action.* Often in a matter of minutes, the money has been spent. There's seldom enough time to think about withdrawing your consent. This phase is usually marked by a brief euphoria: *Wait until your partner sees this great outfit! Wow, won't you enjoy these new CDs!*

4. *Reckoning.* The momentary high has passed, and you're overcome with feelings of guilt, shame, self-hate, hopelessness, and helplessness. How could you do this again? Won't you ever be able to control yourself? Your partner will have a fit when he or she finds out!

5. *Letdown.* You're right back where you started, feeling unhappy, empty, and depressed. Not only that, but you're now deeper in debt, and you may be afraid your partner will be disappointed and lose respect—and love—for you.

Proponents of twelve-step programs such as Debtors Anonymous and Gamblers Anonymous say that admitting one's inability to control compulsive behavior is the first stage of a healing process that will be less dominated by crippling guilt and self-hate. On the other hand, those who are critical of twelve-step programs say they make

Can You Control Your Urge to Spend Without Help?

people feel powerless, robbing them of the self-confidence and self-control they must assert to change their lives. By surrendering to a Higher Power for help, these critics say, spenders give up the responsibility for their choices.

I believe this debate is less important than determining what works best for you as an individual. To determine whether a twelve-step program might work as part of your recovery process, ask yourself these questions:

* When you think your behavior might be something you can't control, like an addiction or a disease, does it motivate you to seek help

from others who have experienced the same thing, or does it make you feel powerless to change what is beyond your control?

✒ Does thinking of overspending as an addiction make you more compassionate toward yourself as you struggle with it, or does it make you feel helpless?

✒ Would you feel support and relief in the company of a group of others who are fighting the same problem? Or would you prefer to work on your recovery privately, perhaps with the help of one or two trusted friends you can open up to?

In my clinical work, I've found that when spenders believe they're suffering from an affliction they can change only with the help of a Higher Power, they often experience an increase in the self-acceptance and compassion necessary to change their lives. As an overspender myself, I accept that the urge to spend sometimes sweeps over me from behind like a tidal wave I can't control. If I slip up, viewing this habit as a compulsion helps me forgive myself and start anew each day to try to nurture myself in deeper ways. For me, it's an ongoing struggle that started when I was very young.

Olivia's Own Story

My mother was a shopaholic. When she felt elated, she'd go shopping. When she felt depressed, she'd go shopping.

She'd come back from one of these binges with shopping bags full of new clothes. She didn't work outside the home at the time and I imagine she felt guilty about spending my father's money this way, because she'd hide the clothes behind the living-room chair until he was in a good mood. Then she'd try on the new purchases one by one, getting enough acceptance from my father to ease her conscience.

As a child, I used to witness these bizarrely predictable rituals, feeling both critical of her and amused at how she was able to relieve her guilt by getting approval from my dad, a loving man but a definite worrier/hoarder. I was involved in this process, too, because my mother's way of showing affection for me was to buy me clothes during one of her spending binges.

"What a great mom!" some of my friends would say, and sigh. It's certainly true that I was spoiled and overindulged in many ways. However, "spoiled" means the same for people as it does for perishables: below the surface, all is not as perfectly healthy as it may seem. In my case, although I appeared to be receiving a lot of attention from my mother, deep inside I was yearning for real approval and love.

Later, when my therapy training helped me to be more objective, I realized that my mother's overspending probably stemmed from the difficulty she had in accepting herself for what she was. For example, her dream was to write the Great American Novel, but she was too paralyzed by her own imperfections to write anything much. Unable to love or be comfortable with herself, she didn't really know how to express in words or hugs the love I needed.

But she did know how to buy me clothes, in large quantities! So although I resented not having the warm, nourishing affection I longed for, I accepted the clothes, reassuring myself as I wore them that they were clearly proof of my mom's love.

After I grew up, started my career as a psychotherapist, and entered my first marriage, it began to dawn on me that whenever I felt lonely or depressed, or whenever I wanted to celebrate, my first impulse was to go out and splurge on clothes for myself. You're probably thinking: *Aha, following in her mother's footsteps!* And you're absolutely right: I'd learned from my mother's example that buying myself clothing was a way to express love.

But what was really astonishing was that I—a working professional with an income equal to my husband's, much of which I managed separately—would find myself hiding my new clothes until he was in a good mood and then trying them on for him before integrating them into my wardrobe!

Not until I started doing "money harmony" work did I understand that I was careening back and forth between my mom's compulsive spendthrift behavior and my dad's compulsive anxiety about spending money. In working with others who learned similar behavior from their parents, relatives, or other influences, I finally was able to confront my feelings and habits squarely enough to begin making a dent in them.

WHEN YOU ALWAYS GET WHAT YOU WANT, YOU MAY NOT GET WHAT YOU NEED

From my own experience, I know that one of the most important lessons children can learn is how to cope with having some of their desires lovingly refused.

Too much deprivation, of course, can make young sufferers unwilling to ever again deny themselves what they want—much like war-wracked Scarlett O'Hara vowing grimly, "As God is my witness, I'll never go hungry again!" But it's equally true that you may grow up unable to tolerate deprivation if you've always been given everything you thought you wanted.

This attitude was already cemented in me by the age of five or six, when my father happened to take me with him to the barbershop where he was to get a haircut. As we were waiting, I saw another child, a boy only a year or two older than I was, ask his father for a quarter. His dad said "No!" in a harsh and dismissive tone of voice, and the boy burst into tears. I was so gripped by that child's overwhelming sense of rejection, deprivation, and misery that I vowed then and there that I would do all in my power to keep from ever feeling as deprived as he did.

I kept that vow, too—largely unconsciously. Whether I had money or not, I acted as if I did. I made the minimum payments on my credit cards for years and tried not to notice how the total balance was ballooning. Whether or not I had enough money for all my wants and needs, I pretended everything was fine—and so I never had to face feeling deprived.

If you grow up with the belief that being denied anything means you're unloved or unlovable, and without understanding that you can survive deprivation, you're a potential overspender ready to be triggered by your paycheck or credit card.

In the real world, of course, you can't always get what you want. If you've become accustomed to instant gratification, you'll rebel when that happens. At the thought of being deprived of what you want, even temporarily, you'll have a tantrum—just like a spoiled kid. Because you're grown up, your tantrum may be internal rather than the kind where you scream or kick your heels on the floor.

My shopping binges for clothing and other self-indulgences were the result of internal "I want it!" tantrums. I was desperately afraid of not being able to cope with any kind of deprivation, emptiness, loneliness, or even the intensity of happy feelings.

I also recognized another unhappy affinity between my mother and myself: She shopped to prove to others that she was an extremely sophisticated and beautiful woman, despite her low self-esteem. On the losing end of this "who's the fairest of them all?" comparison, I grew up feeling like an ugly duckling—and so I

shopped, as she had, for the clothes and cosmetics that would confirm to others that I was attractive and interesting.

NEVER UNDERESTIMATE THE POWER OF AN OVERSPENDER'S PARTNER

As the years passed and I struggled with my overspending, I was
fortunate enough to develop a second long-term relationship—this
time with a healing partner who was very sane and balanced about
money and not judgmental about my own lack of balance in this
area.

Three years after meeting, we married. As I look back at the
evolution of our relationship, I appreciate how much he has helped
me evolve toward money harmony as a recovering (I never say "recovered"!) overspender.

When we first got together, I insisted on keeping most of my
money separate, both to protect my financial independence and to
avoid polluting our relationship with my overspending. Michael
knew I'd previously racked up large credit-card debts, and he said
very simply and straightforwardly, "Honey, it makes no sense to
pay 18 percent a month to credit-card companies. Pay off your
credit cards every month, and if you can't, tell me right away and
I'll help you with it."

If you're ready to change your habits, sometimes all it takes is
good advice like this, offered in a neutral way. His suggestion made
total sense to me, and once I got over the embarrassment of having
illogically let my interest charges mount up, I started paying off my
credit cards regularly. Since we've been together, there have been
a few instances where my expenses have exceeded my income, and
Michael has lent a hand for a short while. But 95 percent of the

time, I've paid off my credit cards promptly and in full. What a relief to have incorporated this piece of financial sanity into my life!

Asked whom we'd be willing to consult for self-improvement advice, many of us would probably put our spouse last on the list. I can understand this perfectly—it's a little risky to put someone who knows your flaws intimately in a position of authority. But in this area of overspending, taking my husband's sound, nonjudgmental advice has worked for me.

The thing I appreciate most about Michael as my ''money mentor'' is that he's helped me balance my moneylife without my ever feeling I've lost his respect. Although he taught me to begin to set limits on myself, partly through his example and partly in our ''moneytalks,'' he has never felt or behaved like my jailer.

For me, our partnership is both healing and empowering. Just as he has taught me to cope with saying no to myself at times and to live well with my money, so have I been able to deepen his appreciation of the power of love, the family, and human relationships. And I know that the hard work I've done in progressing toward money harmony was made easier by his help and support.

In my workshops, seminars, and in this book, I've been candid about this experience for two reasons. First, to reassure you that you're not alone. I understand what an overspender's world is like. I also know that this compulsion can be so deeply rooted as to seem irrational and incomprehensible, as it was to me for a long time.

But the second reason I've told this story is to give you hope. Despite the pressures that may have helped shape your spending habits as you grew up, you can recover. Your strongest ally can be a partner willing to share your struggle and explore his or her own money attitudes to help your relationship rebalance and move toward money harmony.

PART TWO

❧

How Spenders' Partners

Can Help

4.

Overspenders and Those

Who Love Them

What happens to a spender in the intimacy of a relationship? If compulsive overspending typically grows out of roots in childhood experiences or money messages from the past and is nurtured by cultural exhortations to consume, how much influence can the spender's partner hope to have on this compulsion? And how do you know when you're helping in your partner's struggle against overspending—and when you may be making things worse?

In this chapter I'll explain how spenders' partners can take a more objective look at their own role in this struggle. The relationship needn't be a romantic one; many of these principles work equally well for money conflicts between business partners or between parents and children.

It's entirely natural to feel eager to confront your overspending partner and start probing for answers right away. However, this problematic behavior didn't develop all at once, and there's seldom a quick way to fix it. The better you understand how it originates and how you yourself may be affecting it, the more prepared you'll be to help figure out just what's out of balance and to work toward a solution with your partner in a healthy, positive way.

> ## Key Questions to Ask Yourself About Your Relationship

It can be tremendously helpful for a caring partner to offer solid support to an overspender. But just what kind of support . . . and how much?

If you've known about your partner's spending problem for a while, you've probably been somewhat perplexed about whether you're reacting the right way. You may even be switching from one kind of behavior to another, confusing the partner you're trying to help, as you wrestle with endless questions you don't know the answers to: Has something you've done provoked this problem or made it worse? Should you be stern, upset, or forgiving? Or should you pretend not to notice? Will your partner straighten out if you just leave him or her alone?

To help you determine the impact you're having on your partner's spending problem, I've identified three major questions you need to answer honestly and courageously. Let's look at them one by one.

> ## How Has Your Partner's Overspending Been Affected by Your Relationship?

This first question has three possible answers: Your partner's overspending has become worse, it has gotten better, or it has remained the same. Your thoughtful response here will help determine whether overspending may be linked to something out of balance in your relationship, whether some positive dynamics between the two of you have already begun to promote healing, or whether the basic problem is largely independent of your partnership.

THE OVERSPENDING HAS BECOME WORSE.

If this is the case, your partner's compulsion to spend—to fill himself or herself up with "things"—may signal some other area(s) of tension in your relationship such as workaholism, sexual problems, poor communication, loneliness, or fear of intimacy.

If you're a hoarder who likes to keep your money under tight control, your closefisted behavior may have turned your partner into a resentful, rebellious (and possibly sneaky) overspender. If you're also openly disapproving of your partner's spending, he or she may feel even more compelled to go out and buy temporary happiness or satisfaction, driven by a motive that can be either "Poor me" or "Screw you."

THE OVERSPENDING HAS GOTTEN BETTER.

You may be helping your overspender partner to recover if you're loving, open, and vulnerable, unafraid to share your own imperfections and struggles (whether money-related or not), and willing to help your partner find nonspending solutions to his or her needs. This support can make it possible for a spender to confront the addiction that prompts him or her to fill up on the empty calories of self-gratification and to replace this compulsion gradually with deeper sources of nourishment.

For tips and exercises to help couples learn how to replenish each other in this way, see Jennifer Louden's wonderful guide *The Couple's Comfort Book: A Creative Guide for Renewing Passion, Pleasure and Commitment*. Harville Hendrix's and John Gray's books are also a gold mine of ideas to help you reromanticize your relationship. (See bibliography.)

THE OVERSPENDING HAS REMAINED THE SAME.

If the spending pattern seems to have a life of its own, unaffected by the warmth and nurturing of your relationship, it's fair to surmise that it's a very old addiction, deeply rooted in childhood deprivation and feelings of emptiness, incompetence, anxiety, or depression. It's crucial for you not to take it personally. Instead, simply view it as a condition—like nearsightedness—that your partner already had when you met each other. In this kind of situation, longer-term help from therapy and support groups such as Debtors Anonymous becomes even more important. You must try to stay detached enough to view your spender partner's efforts with compassion. Often, a sensible first step is to separate your finances, so you won't have the worry of your own money being held hostage to your partner's success or failure. By protecting yourself lovingly but firmly, you'll have more love and acceptance to give your struggling partner. (In the next chapter, we'll discuss this at greater length.)

In my work with overspenders, I've uncovered four myths that often derail
partners like you from providing the
love and support your spender partner
needs. Although each myth has some
elements of truth in it, each also con-
tains dangerous distortions. Have any
of these myths been influencing your
behavior?

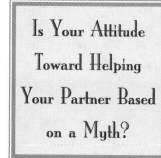

Is Your Attitude
Toward Helping
Your Partner Based
on a Myth?

"TRUE LOVE CAN CONQUER ALL"

Do you believe that if you just loved your partner enough, he or she
would stop overspending?

As we've seen, overspending usually has very deep roots that
go much farther back than the start of your relationship—to ado-
lescence or childhood. Even if you love your partner very much and
try hard to please him or her, the overspending will probably persist until the spender is willing to confront it and work on digging
down to its roots.

"I CAN CHANGE WHAT'S WRONG AND MAKE MY PARTNER STOP HURTING"

*Maybe if I didn't work so hard . . . or if we went out to dinner more
often . . . or if I made more money. . . .* You can spend hours won-
dering just what you're guilty of doing (or not doing) that compels
your partner to seek refuge in shopping.

It's true that overspending-prone partners often buy more when they feel lonely, abandoned, angry, frustrated, sexually or emotionally starved, or unfulfilled. However, the deep roots of this behavior mean that it's apt to continue even if the immediate source of dissatisfaction is remedied (your heavy travel schedule, for example). Recovery must start with the spender learning to understand and change his or her behavior patterns. While this hard work is under way, you may be able to help a great deal by being more attentive to your partner's needs—but you can't singlehandedly solve the underlying problem.

"IT'S USELESS TO TRY TO HELP"

Though overspending is the spender's problem, it's not true that there's nothing you can do. You can help your partner take the essential steps of healing by working together to understand this mysterious compulsion and to identify some of the sources of emptiness and deprivation that are fueling it. Your partner may also be glad of your help in planning ways to resist temptation and working out alternatives to spending that will fulfill his or her real, deeper needs.

"IF I GET TOO CLOSE, WE'LL END UP STRUGGLING IN THE TAR PIT TOGETHER"

This is a tricky one. It's true that if you involve yourself too deeply in your partner's effort, you lose the detached compassion and caring that can be so helpful. In fact, you become vulnerable to an addiction of your own: the need to be needed or to control. Many therapists term this loss of detachment *codependency*.[1]

For example, you may become codependent if you take over all the family money and dole it out to your spender partner with strict instructions on how it's to be spent. Although it may seem that you're only trying to help an overspender avoid temptation, what you're really doing is keeping your partner dependent on you, so you'll be able to continue taking care of him or her. To feel balanced and self-confident, your partner must have the opportunity to learn disciplined spending habits independently, which won't happen if you continue to spoon-feed him or her like a helpless infant.

Codependency may also result when you're so intimately involved in your partner's recovery process that his or her journey becomes your own: You're constantly urging the spender to be "good," and feel upset and angry if progress is intermittent or slow.

Try not to invest yourself so deeply in the recovery program that you feel you've failed if your partner doesn't succeed quickly. It's better to focus on keeping an open dialogue so you know how the struggle is going and what your partner is feeling and coping with. Weekly moneytalks can be an excellent caring (but non-smothering) way to stay in touch.

And by all means, do whatever you can to help your partner feel fulfilled, without compromising your own needs and self-interest. For example, you might set aside some quality time every week for intimate conversations or romantic dates.

Keeping the right distance may seem like walking a tightrope—and in a way, it's just that. If you're too remote, your partner may feel alone and unsupported. If you're too involved, it may appear that you're nagging, breathing down your partner's neck, or trying to take over. In short, learning to support and encourage without becoming either codependent or aloof is a skill that will take a good deal of practice.

These four myths are so common that you needn't feel embarrassed if you've believed in any of them. By analyzing them carefully, I've tried to give you a more realistic sense of your limited ability to solve your partner's overspending all by yourself. This doesn't mean you're powerless, just that you can only help your partner if he or she is already committed to making a personal journey toward healing. In other words, the spender—not you—must be the prime mover in the recovery process.

Are Your Money Attitudes Making You Part of the Problem?

So far, we've explored the change (or lack of change) in your partner's overspending while you've been together, and your feelings about your own role in solving this behavior problem. Although you may not know yet what long-held money messages lie at the root of this behavior (an investigation we'll undertake in chapter 9), it can be worthwhile to examine exactly what kind of war the two of you might be waging.

There are two likely reasons for friction in your money relationship: First, you're different money types, and/or second, you have different priorities. Sounds like the same thing, doesn't it? But understanding the distinction may bring you much closer to resolving your conflict.

"DUEL" PERSONALITIES

Based on what you've read in this book so far, you may feel fairly certain your partner is a spender. If so, are you a hoarder, or are you a spender, too? Are you mild or extreme spenders or hoarders?

As we've discussed, most couples tend to become polarized in their attitudes toward money. Even if they weren't opposites when they met (and they often are), eventually they'll modify their habits to counterbalance each other's behavior. This reaction may be mild or extreme, depending on how convinced they are that their partner's actions will endanger the financial balance of the relationship.

Thus, the partner of a overspender may become an extreme hoarder to keep them from being swamped with debt. Although the couple may indeed remain solvent (an outcome by no means guaranteed), balancing acts like this are often achieved at the cost of tremendous internal friction between two radically different money types—literally "duel" personalities.

* If an *avoider* forgets to pay bills and never knows where the money goes, the other partner typically develops into a *worrier*, trying anxiously to keep track of income and outgo.

* A partner with *money monk* tendencies, who believes the love of money is the root of all evil (and hence feels uncomfortable having too much of it), may help create an *amasser*, who enjoys the feelings of success and power which come from accumulating money.

* In investment matters, an aggressive *risk taker* is usually balanced by a more conservative *risk avoider*. This polarization often runs along gender lines, with men generally being more eager to take risks than women.

❧ When one partner is a *planner*, strategizing and mapping out the couple's joint financial future to the last detail, the other is often a *dreamer*—an impulsive, sometimes impractical visionary.

Of course, there are cases where this polarization doesn't occur. Two hoarders, for example, may be perfectly happy together if neither ever feels an urge to buy more than the necessities of life. It's less common to find two spenders together, since one of them usually has to move toward a saving position if they're not to go broke within a few credit-card billing cycles.

Remember, it's not inherently good or bad to be a spender or a hoarder, an avoider or a worrier; each of these roles has positive and negative aspects. In fact, my therapy work with couples suggests that troublesome negative qualities are often the flip side of the positive qualities that initially attracted you to your partner— like Rita's discovery that the lavish spending with which Brian had charmed and flattered her during courtship began to hurt their savings program after they were married.

If you see your basic problem as a conflict of different money types, you need to ask yourself one more question: Is the conflict in your relationship truly and totally due to overspending behavior by your partner?

Here's why this question is important: If you see your partner as an overspender, you've probably experienced a lot of discord already. In fact, there's a good chance the two of you have had emotionally charged arguments. Your partner may have denied being extravagant, insisting that his or her spending is relatively normal. You may have been accused of being stingy and tight, and of having no idea how much things cost these days—implying that you're the one who's out of balance.

And there may be some truth in this charge. If you're a superfrugal hoarder who avoids spending money on any immediate pleasures, it's entirely possible that you may see your partner as a spendthrift even if he or she is just spending normally.

Obviously, it can be helpful to know where you really stand, if for no other reason than to know how far you yourself may be from a middle position—the balance point of the money harmony you hope to achieve as a couple.

You're already familiar with my quiz to help verify whether or not a person is an overspender. Here's its counterpart for hoarders.

ARE YOU A HOARDER?

1. Does it bother you to spend money impulsively on some nonessential purchase to please yourself or a loved one?

2. Do you go to great lengths to save even small amounts of money, no matter how much time and effort it takes? (For example, do you regularly travel miles out of your way to your bank's free ATM, rather than use a nearer money machine that charges a $1 fee?)

3. Do you begrudge your partner almost any expenditure of money?

4. Do you have the feeling that no matter how much you save, it will never be enough?

5. Do you deny yourself and your loved ones expensive gifts or luxury purchases, no matter what the occasion is or how much money you have available?

6. Do you feel happiest and most secure when you're not spending any money at all?

7. Do you insist on buying the most inexpensive version of something you need, even if this choice may not really be the best value in the

long run? (For example, would you be apt to buy a cheap telephone, knowing it might not hold up as well as a more expensive one?)

If you answered *yes* to at least four of these questions, you may be a compulsive saver, resistant to spending money on all but the most vital necessities. It's possible that your attitude has prompted your partner's spending behavior to become more extreme, a way of rebelling against your attempts to control the money and dictate what it may be spent on.

Besides potentially causing your spender partner to overreact, your hoarder perspective will make it doubly hard for you to understand the inner world of the spender and to know what must change so he or she can move toward more balanced money habits. Unless you reassess your own behavior and learn to communicate with empathy about the differences in your respective viewpoints, you won't be able to heal these rifts. In fact, they'll deepen and intensify over time.

Thus, if the two of you are divided by different beliefs about money, your task must be, first and foremost, to work on your own issues, instead of focusing your initial energy on what your partner should do to change.

CONFLICTING PRIORITIES

Your chronic fights or underlying tensions also may be due to something other than polarized money beliefs. Maybe you simply have different priorities about how to spend your money.

In fact, discord due to different priorities can exist with or without overspending. If you've already identified a definite spending problem, take the time to consider whether a difference in priorities may be adding to your difficulty. For example, does one of you want to spend your money buying, restoring, and reselling classic motorcycles, while the other insists on socking every spare penny into a tax-sheltered retirement plan? If this kind of dissension seems to be part of your conflict, work to uncover and identify your different priorities so they don't complicate your attempt to deal with the more fundamental issue of overspending.

On the other hand, if you and your partner tend not to butt heads over the issue of "spend" versus "save," there's a good chance your problem isn't your money beliefs at all, just your priorities. If so, the solution may be simpler, since it's usually much easier to change what we do than what we believe in.

To identify and resolve your different priorities, try to get to the bottom of each other's need by open communication and respectful listening, as Ron and Sylvia did in the following example.

Sylvia and Ron began therapy because they fought constantly about money. Some people might have wondered how money could possibly be a big problem for this thirtysomething couple. With a combined income of more than $100,000, no serious debt, and no children, they both seemed to be comfortable with spending their

> **Building Bridges:
> The Story of
> Ron and Sylvia**

disposable income on things they wanted.

The problem was their differing priorities. Ron preferred to spend the money on his sailboat and on expensive vacations, while Sylvia wanted to spend it on their home. Unlike Sylvia, Ron wasn't bothered by the shabbiness of their existing furniture. "We don't need a new couch!" he protested. Unlike Ron, Sylvia couldn't see the value of buying a new spinnaker for his sloop. "I feel like you're escaping from me to that sailboat," she complained.

My therapy with them consisted mainly of giving them tools to encourage a calm and empathetic dialogue, so each could learn to recognize and respect the other's underlying needs. Although Ron admitted he sometimes did use the sailboat to escape closeness with his wife, in a larger sense it helped satisfy his inner need for freedom and adventure. Sylvia revealed that because of childhood insecurities about being poorer and less acceptable than her neighbors and peers, she now gained pleasure and fulfillment from having a home full of beautiful things where she could be proud to entertain friends and family.

As they came to appreciate and respect each other's very different needs, Ron and Sylvia began to work together to figure out solutions that would eventually satisfy both of them. Each became more willing to defer personal gratification for a time, for the sake of their ultimate mutual harmony.

Most often, when partners want to spend money on different things, these needs aren't in direct opposition. Win/win solutions can result from empathetic communication, careful listening, clear negotiation, and a willingness to compromise on timetables so each partner's needs can eventually be met.

As we're seeing, overspenders aren't born, they're made—by their experiences growing up, by the attitudes of the authority figures in their young lives, by a society that makes spending easy and acceptable. Probably not by you—and certainly not by you alone.

But you can make a difference. In a close relationship, the attitude partners take can drive spenders to more desperate behavior if they're unhappy, or help them to heal if they're ready. That's why I've taken this time to help you understand your own role a little better. In the next chapters, we'll look at how you can use this self-knowledge in a productive way to understand and help your partner recover from overspending.

5.

How Can You Help

in a Healthy Way?

We've all watched, enthralled, cheering over our popcorn, as the caped superhero zooms out of nowhere to scoop his (or her) beloved out of the clutches of a dastardly villain. It's just a short step from that silver-screen scenario to one in which we envision ourselves, selfless and invincible, swooping in to rescue the partner we love from the ravenous monster of overspending.

I believe you really can help vanquish the monster . . . though not quite that easily, and not by yourself. As an overspender's partner, you've been cast for Best Supporting Role—a title that, if all goes well, will be gratefully awarded to you by the real hero or heroine of this drama: your partner.

Supportive

Detachment

In the last chapter, we looked at the difficulty of being caring, yet objective. There's a real danger that if you become too closely involved with your partner's struggle, you'll try to take over the fight yourself, preventing your partner from developing the strength he or she needs in order to heal.

This is what therapists specializing in addiction recovery call *enabling*. Ironically, the more you care for your partner, the likelier you are to enable their addiction by trying to make the hard choices easier for them. An example might be if you constantly bail your partner out whenever he or she overspends ("It's okay, honey, I know you couldn't help it. I'll write a check to cover the payment"). Or if you become the Comptroller of the Currency, sometimes withholding money and other times giving your partner permission to spend ("I know you've had a rough week. Why don't you go ahead and buy yourself those shoes you've been talking about?").

On the other hand, you can be involved, supportive, and healing without having to race to the rescue in your Superman or Wonder Woman suit every time your partner strays from the straight and narrow. It may be difficult at first, but you must steel yourself to be able to witness an occasional slip or stumble in your partner's struggle to heal without feeling it's a personal defeat or a slap in your face.

Try not to get too deeply wrapped up in the importance of constant progress. No graphs, no charts, no gold stars for good behavior. If your partner feels motivated by such symbols of progress, let him or her keep track of them. You just need to be there with your support, and provide firm, loving help in setting limits.

Remember, setting limits doesn't mean you get to be the budgetmeister, dictating what gets spent, where, when, and by whom. To be effective, limits must be mutually agreed on by both you and your spender partner. For example, the two of you might negotiate that your partner will have total discretion in spending a certain limited amount of money every week, without any judgment from you. This helps the spender practice disciplined freedom. And because it's a contract of trust between the two of you, the spender is usually much more willing to abide by it than if you'd issued a unilateral decree ("You absolutely can't spend another penny! You're driving us to the poorhouse!").

If you find yourself reacting too strongly to your partner's day-to-day progress as time goes on, it means you've gotten too enmeshed in the struggle. Step back, breathe deeply, center yourself, and give your partner the space he or she needs, even though it may well mean a step back for every two steps forward. It's both natural and normal for progress toward growth to be halting, especially at first.

Even if your partner seems to lose heart or run out of steam, don't give up. Just be there, ready with healthy detachment and loving and compassionate support for the moment when he or she decides to take up the challenge again. Only then will you feel you've done your best to make the relationship work.

Separate accounts can be a useful way to protect your financial security, retain your objectivity, and reduce conflict while the two of you are working to solve a serious overspending problem.

Sensible Self-Defense: Separating Your Finances

As radical a step as this may seem, it's often the best way of keeping yourself from becoming too deeply invested (literally) in your partner's recovery process. If every step backward wounds you in the wallet, you'll never be able to maintain the compassionate detachment necessary to help your partner heal.

Also, this move sends an important signal to the spender: that you aren't willing to be codependent, enabling his or her compulsion with continual bailouts. Your partner will undoubtedly feel angry, rejected, or even abandoned by this drastic action, but if the problem is severe enough, it's really the wisest choice for you both. If you keep rushing to the rescue every time your partner gets into deep financial waters, he or she will never learn to swim, and you'll be too exhausted and anxious (and/or angry and resentful) to provide the steady support and caring that are vitally needed.

SCENARIO 1: IF YOU EARN MUCH MORE THAN YOUR OVERSPENDING PARTNER

If your partner otherwise wouldn't have the funds to live in reasonable comfort and financial security, consider working out an arrangement to supplement his or her income with a fixed contribution from you.

If the lower-income overspender is your wife, with primary responsibility for child raising, I strongly recommend that you compensate her for her crucial family responsibilities. If the concept of paying her a salary feels too impersonal, find some other way to supplement her income so you can move toward a better balance of financial power.

If the lower-paid overspender is your husband or male partner, I also suggest trying to equalize the income more—perhaps with a salary or supplemental income recognizing his contributions to household maintenance and repair. (I don't mean to stereotype anyone with these generalities. If your partner is a Mr. Mom, more financial power to him! Or if she's Ms. Goodwrench, keeping the family cars in A-1 shape, count your blessings.)

SCENARIO 2: IF YOU EARN LESS THAN YOUR OVERSPENDING PARTNER

If your own income is too low to cover your basic needs, you're highly vulnerable to a spendthrift partner's extravagance. To assure yourself of the financial and emotional security you need, try to work out a deal with your better-paid partner to provide a regular allowance or salary (especially if you bear a bigger share of the family responsibilities).

The most trouble-free arrangement might be direct deposits from your partner's paycheck into a bank account held in your name alone. This way, your money's protected because the spender never really has access to it. (With your partner's consent, his or her bank or employer can usually set this up.)

GETTING YOUR PARTNER'S AGREEMENT TO SEPARATE YOUR MONEY

How do you introduce such a potentially explosive topic as dividing your finances?

I recommend choosing a time when overspending isn't a hot issue (in other words, *not* while you're in the middle of an argument about the bills) and inviting your partner to sit down with you. Present your firm but loving request for separate finances as something you need to do; otherwise, you won't feel safe enough to be supportive as your partner confronts the spending problem. In an extreme case of escalating debt, this move may be the only way to protect yourself from becoming so financially frightened that separation or divorce becomes the only solution.

Anticipating that your partner will at first feel lonely and abandoned and may be quite upset, you should be especially careful to communicate in a compassionate and nonpunitive way. If the subject is difficult for you, and/or if you feel bad about making your partner unhappy, say so—but emphasize that you feel compelled to propose this step so you can stay detached enough to continue being loving, caring, and supportive.

Once these separate arrangements have been made, don't get in the habit of bailing out your overspending partner. Though he or she may even have a tantrum at some point about your refusal to come to the rescue ("If you really loved me, you'd help me out of this jam!"), in the long run a recovering spender will come to appreciate your loving refusal as support in his or her fight against this compulsion.

Separate money may also be a good solution if you and your partner are prone to turf disputes arising from a deeply felt need for financial independence—as in this young couple's case.

Don't Fence Me In: The Story of Jeanne and Carl

Carl and Jeanne couldn't seem to stop fighting over the most commonplace money matter: balancing the checkbook. Both young professionals who made good salaries, they were trying to keep track of their spending in a responsible way by meeting once a week with their check stubs, ATM slips, and debit-card receipts to bring the checkbook up to date. However, their get-togethers often turned into confrontations if Carl commented on or questioned Jeanne's purchases. Feeling she was being criticized for overspending, Jeanne reacted with hostility, accusing Carl of trying to control everything.

Further discussion revealed that Jeanne's hypersensitivity to her husband's questions had its roots in the past. As a girl, she'd been required by her father to detail how she planned to spend every dollar of her allowance before he'd grant her the money. Now, even a simple inquiry from Carl about her spending triggered memories of these humiliating cross-examinations—and to make matters worse, now she was being grilled about money that was partly hers to begin with!

Although Jeanne might ordinarily have been a mild spender, her conflict with Carl (a mild hoarder) was aggravated by these childhood memories. When it seemed to her that Carl was trying to dictate her spending as her father had, she rebelled by becoming an even more extreme spender.

I suggested that this friction might be reduced if she kept her money separate and managed it by herself. The solution eventually agreed to by Carl and Jeanne was a simple one: She would keep her income in a separate account and write a check to her husband every month for her share of the household expenses. With this step, Jeanne's rebellious overspending diminished, and the money battles undermining her relationship with Carl ceased.

> Separate Money Can Make Even a Balanced Relationship Stronger

Even in the absence of a spending problem, keeping some money separate often helps individual partners to retain a healthy sense of autonomy, encouraging a fusion of independence and interdependence that can make a relationship even stronger.

In my experience of working with committed couples, a man typically resists the idea of separate accounts far more than a woman does, perhaps because he feels she's rejecting his willingness to share everything with her. It's important for a husband to understand that his wife's need for money of her own does *not* mean she doesn't love or trust him, or that she's contemplating divorce. Raised to share and merge herself with others (as most women are), she may simply be expressing the important need to retain some "unmerged" identity and choices of her own.

As you may have noticed when I described my relationships in chapter 3, I feel more comfortable keeping at least some of my money separate. Originally this was in part to set limits on my overspending—a motive that is less important now. But apart from the practical importance of maintaining a credit history in one's own name, like many other women I value the sense of autonomy that comes from having control of my money. This financial independence isn't really a practical necessity, since I can imagine very few things Michael would seriously object to my spending "our" money on. But because having separate money makes me feel healthily responsible for myself, and helps me value and respect my own abilities when I manage it sensibly, I believe it's an important part of the money harmony in our relationship.

Merged money is actually a fairly recent development. Wealthy women almost always kept control of their fortunes themselves. And for a long time, it was customary for stay-at-home wives to be paid a housekeeping allowance by their working husbands, theirs to spend or save as they saw fit. Just as often, a man would come home from the mill or the factory and hand his wife his paycheck— and then *he'd* get an allowance while she handled the household finances. It was only when these couples' daughters hung up their aprons, buttoned their power suits, and joined the workforce that it began to be assumed that their money would be merged with their husband's.

This arrangement works fine for some couples. For others— particularly if one partner isn't willing to give up the freedom and control of managing his or her own money—it can make good sense to have separate discretionary accounts, along with a joint housekeeping account out of which the mortgage and other household expenses are paid and to which each partner contributes equally (or proportionate to his or her income, if that's fairer).

There are no hard and fast rules; the arrangement doesn't even have to be symmetrical. One partner may want a discretionary account, while the other agrees to handle all the other money. So if you think separating "your" from "his" or "her" money might help reduce the nuclear chain reaction that has been pushing your relationship toward meltdown, feel free to set up whatever works for the two of you.

As we've seen, detachment doesn't mean you don't care. On the contrary, it means you care enough to want your partner to grow by exercising his or her own courage, tenacity, and willingness to

Respecting Your Partner's Right to Responsibility

change. If you involve yourself too deeply in this struggle, you may cheat your partner of the right to be responsible for his or her own choices—and prevent the growth that will create a happier, better balanced human being.

In my opinion, there are two facets to helping your partner in a healthy way. First, you need to learn to protect yourself by keeping your partner's struggle at arm's length. Second, you must also be willing to observe that struggle with understanding, compassion, and respect—so that at the right time, those arms can reach out with a pat on the back, a gentle nudge, or a warm and loving hug.

Long-haul Helping Strategies

As an overspender's partner, there are many specific ways you can provide support and encouragement to make your pilgrim's difficult progress a little less lonely. Many of these strategies dovetail with efforts the spender will be undertaking, letting you work together to help each other—and your relationship—continue moving toward money harmony over the long term.

WORK WITH YOUR PARTNER TO SET A FINANCIAL GOAL YOU BOTH WANT

Let your partner take the lead in suggesting specific goals that would motivate him or her to forgo the satisfaction of spending. If you're a saver by nature, be prepared to find your spender partner isn't turned on by such sensible but intangible goals as a retirement nest egg, an emergency savings account, or even a college fund for the kids. You're most apt to agree on goals that offer on-the-spot rewards as well as long-term value, but don't be too adamant in resisting a target your partner is set on. (Remember, the discipline of postponing gratification is valuable in itself. And after all, it's better to finance a desired item with savings than to go into debt to pay for it.)

Once you've settled on your goal, keep some highly visible reminder of it where the whole family will be aware of it. For example, decorate the family room with a sun-drenched travel poster promoting your planned vacation in Barbados, or post a regularly updated chart on the refrigerator that tracks the growth of your summer-camp savings account for the kids.

HELP YOUR PARTNER MEET HIS OR HER DEEPER NEEDS

Once your partner has begun to uncover the needs that underlie the urge to spend (or at least the circumstances that appear to trigger it), ask what you can do to help and support the healing process. Here are some suggestions:

- More romantic dates together.

- Weekend getaways without the kids.

- Allowing the spender more private time by himself (or herself).

- More sharing of thoughts, feelings, and needs with each other.

- More pleasurable or sensual lovemaking. (Try music, massage, a favorite scent, a different time of day.)

- A quiet "attitude adjustment" cuddle every evening, just holding each other for ten or twenty minutes while you tell each other about your respective days.

* Spending a few minutes every day talking about something you appreciate about each other, in as much detail as you can.

Though you can't meet all of your partner's needs (and shouldn't expect to), your support in activities like these can aid the spender's struggle to recover while helping you grow closer as a couple.

MAKE IT EASIER FOR YOUR PARTNER TO HELP HIMSELF OR HERSELF

There are many specific ways you can contribute directly or indirectly to the healing process. We've touched on some of them already, but here's a brief summary.

* Do what you can to arrange your schedule so your partner can attend support-group meetings or therapy sessions. Taking responsibility for the kids for a couple of hours a week or doing the grocery shopping is a small price to pay to help your partner's healing.

* Make time for your partner to share his or her struggles, progress, temptations, and setbacks. You can be a real source of support if you remember to listen empathetically and keep a healthy distance, refraining from jumping in with unsolicited advice or criticism. If your partner would rather not talk about how it's going, respect his or her need for privacy in the midst of this wrenching change. (Try not to take this reticence too personally; it's more likely to reflect the spender's shame or vulnerability than any distrust of you as a listener.)

* Help your partner think of rewards for taking new actions. These should be more deeply nourishing and satisfying alternatives to compulsive shopping, as we will discuss in chapter 10.

LOOK BEFORE YOU LEAP INTO
SETTING LIMITS

I know you're tempted to "help" your partner by playing a parental role in determining how much he or she should spend. But beware before you take on this job, for there are two pitfalls you may
stumble into.

The first is a danger to yourself that Lord Acton tersely summa-
rized as "Power tends to corrupt." Especially if you've been a controlling type of hoarder in the past, you'll be tempted to clutch
the purse strings extra tightly, feeling authorized to do so by your
partner's obvious struggle. This overcontrolling behavior will end
up hurting you by pushing your attitude toward money even further out of balance.

Second—and more important—it won't really help your partner. If you take over all the spending decisions, you'll thwart the
recovery process by preventing your partner from making the
choices that can build up his or her responsibility, confidence, and
self-esteem.

Having made this point, I would add that there may be excep-
tions under certain circumstances. If your partner asks you at the
very beginning of the recovery program to help set limits and actively participate in encouraging him or her to stick to them . . .
and if you feel you can be a loving, nonjudgmental limit setter . . .
then you might consider handling this role for a short time until
your partner is strong enough to take it over. As I mentioned earlier
in discussing helping vs. enabling, your goal should be to help your
partner develop the muscle he or she will need to change the habits
of a lifetime. Don't become so involved in making his or her choices
easier that you become locked into caretaking and/or controlling.

It might help to think of yourself as a coach. You can't throw
the ball or sprint over the hurdles for your partner—only he or she

can make the life changes needed to overcome overspending. But you can be there to provide encouragement in times of trial, understanding and support in moments of disappointment or despondency, and congratulations in times of triumph.

AVOID RUSHING REPEATEDLY TO
YOUR PARTNER'S RESCUE

Keep that cape and those spangled tights in the closet! If you regularly bail out your overspender, you deny him or her the opportunity to grow and heal by taking personal responsibility for money choices and decisions.

It's probably okay to float a modest short-term loan if unforeseeable circumstances occur (like a late paycheck), but for the sake of your partner's self-esteem, make sure you're paid back promptly, with no excuses. If this doesn't happen, you'd better close your lending office. Unless the spender can learn the hard way to exercise disciplined behavior around money, he or she will never gain the self-respect needed to experience real money harmony.

BE PATIENT WITH INEVITABLE
SETBACKS

You don't have to enjoy relapses, but it's important not to overreact when they occur. (Having separate money should help keep you from panicking.) Simply view them as temporary, and a natural part of the recovery process.

When you try to stay detached in this way, it's easier to stand by and wait until your partner is ready to get back on track. You might ask if there's anything you can do to help him or her return to the recovery program. If the answer is *no*, don't rush things. Respect your partner's need for privacy while he or she seeks the way back.

RECOGNIZE AND HONOR EVEN
SMALL SIGNS OF PROGRESS

These little seedlings of change need to be tended with care and love if they're to grow and blossom. You could say something like "I notice you bought the video of that Kevin Costner movie, but took it back a few days later. I think that's great, honey. How's it been for you lately, now that you're trying to spend less money on videos?"

SHARE YOUR OWN STRUGGLES
AND VULNERABILITIES

Remember that it helps your partner not to feel singled out as the "identified patient" of the family. Keep sharing your own struggles with the issues that are troubling you, whether they're related to money or to another area like work, friendships, weight, food, or perfectionism. You could also tell your partner about some of your unmet needs that he or she might be willing to fulfill.

This sharing will help remove the uncomfortable perception that your partner is one-down and you're one-up. Furthermore, it will promote your own self-awareness and growth, and encourage more closeness in your relationship. Your partner will feel less alone, ashamed, and exposed, and more like a participant in a process of mutual self-development and self-improvement.

HOMEWORK EXERCISES FOR
HOARDERS

> **≈** Cut out one habit which requires spending a lot of time or other resources to save a little money. For example: driving miles to an out-of-the-way gas station to save a few pennies a gallon.

> **≈** Award yourself a weekly allowance (perhaps $10 to $25) to be spent solely on things to give yourself or your loved ones pleasure.

> **≈** Buy one "luxury" item which is outside your budget but useful and affordable.

> **≈** Make a list of people you know who enjoy their money in the present, while still managing to prepare for their financial future.

> **≈** Write weekly money dialogues to track your changing attitude toward money.

Admittedly, it's a tall order. If your partner is asking for help in setting limits but you don't wish to take on the task, you might suggest a friend who's willing to act as a money mentor. Chronic overspenders can often benefit from ongoing therapy with a professional trained in money issues. The regular monitoring and emotional support of a group like Debtors Anonymous (DA) may also help them stay on track. In fact, many overspenders find recovery easier through a combination of therapy, DA, and the support of someone they love and trust.

6.

Breaking the Bonds of

Secrecy and Shame

Without light and fresh air, wounds seldom heal—yet it's extraordinarily difficult to be open about one's compulsive behavior. Bound by feelings of shame and defensiveness, spenders may resist admitting to themselves, to you, or to others who can help them that a problem even exists.

To help your partner confront and overcome overspending, you need to understand attitudes that may block his or her acknowledgment of the situation. In this chapter, I'll help you recognize the obstacles to openness you're likeliest to encounter. You'll also find suggestions on how to help your partner break through these barriers and begin the recovery process.

Remember, though, that you can't help by forcing a confrontation with your partner. Don't say, "Look, I know you're denying (or hiding, or even lying about) your spending problem. Face it, you need help!" This scolding or condemnatory attitude is apt to make the spender lash back in defensive hostility or shrink even deeper into a shell of shame, guilt, and unhappiness.

Be as tactful and nonjudgmental as you can—and let your partner take the lead in overcoming any of these barriers that may stand in the way of openness.

Gender-Typical Reactions

In chapter 2, I noted that men and women often behave differently when confronted with a partner's concern that their spending is disrupting the relationship. Women tend to be immediately overwhelmed by feelings of shame, guilt, and rejection, which they may either turn on themselves or invert into an explosive backlash against the partner they feel is persecuting them.

Starting a dialogue with a male overspender can be difficult, too, since most men hate to admit they're incompetent or wrong, especially when it comes to money management—a subject traditionally considered within the male domain of expertise.

When men and women have money conflicts, it often happens that the man blames the woman, and the woman blames herself. If the woman explodes in a defensive counterattack, both of them may blame each other. The dialogue may sound like this:

HE: I'm working at an armpit of a job because I can't afford to quit, and you go out and spend $40 on a new bedspread. For pete's sake! Where do you think our money comes from, the tooth fairy?

SHE: Honey, I've been trying hard to be careful and not buy anything we don't need, but this was such a great deal. . . . Never mind, you're right. You work hard for our money, and I guess I just wasn't thinking. I'm sorry.

Or like this:

SHE: I know how much you've wanted a notebook computer, but we just don't have the money. Maybe I shouldn't have turned down that overtime last week.

HE: Sweetheart, you're always saying we never have the money for anything. We've got two incomes—what the heck do you want to do with it all? Save it for our old age?

SHE: Since you mention it, yes! I thought we agreed we were going to max out our IRAs this year. The way you've been spending lately, we'll never be able to save the money by tax time!

Instead of getting mad, a spender may decide to get even by acting cold and hostile, rebuffing a partner's sexual overtures, rejecting attempts to restore closeness in a friendship or good relations in a business partnership, or even acting out the behavior he or she is under attack for. For example, a spender may say to herself, "I'm sick and tired of being made to feel like I can't even afford a new pair of panty hose. I'm going out and buying what I darn well please!"

If you're caught up in one of these gender-related "who's to blame" games, call a time-out. Remember that your respective money styles have been influenced by each other's behavior as you've instinctively sought to balance one another—so no one is completely to blame for what's happening now, or what occurred in the past. The question is what you're going to do about the future.

Shame

Shame is the emotion we feel if who we are, or what we've done, doesn't measure up to our ideal view of ourselves. Most of us have something in our lives that we feel ashamed of and would be mortified to reveal to others. Our worst fear is that if people find out this terrible thing about us, they'll be disappointed in us, despise us, reject us, or even abandon us.

The paradox is that we can only heal ourselves of shame by holding it up to the light—first by facing the truth ourselves and then by finding the courage to share it with others, so we can see we really won't lose their respect or their acceptance.

One of the reasons why groups like Debtors Anonymous are so effective is that they help people confront and overcome feelings of shame. There's something oddly healing about saying to a group of sympathetic strangers, "Hello, I'm _____, and I'm a compulsive debtor." Though it may sound humiliating and indeed makes you feel very vulnerable, there's an element of surrender that brings relief—relief from endlessly trying to hide from your imperfections.

If you believe feelings of shame may be preventing your partner from coming to grips with a spending problem, you can help by making it safe for him or her to share these feelings with you. For example, after asking for a few private moments to discuss something important, you might say gently and compassionately, "Honey, you're one of the most sensitive people I know. I'm hoping you're as concerned as I am about how much money we've been spending lately. I know this is a difficult area for us. Would you be willing to talk about what we can do about it? Let's agree from the start that we won't blame each other, just try to work together on a solution."

Like others who suffer from compulsive addictions,[1] overspenders often live in a fog of denial. They pay the minimum balance on their monthly credit-card bills without thinking about the double-digit interest rate, juggle other bills

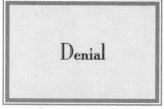

Denial

to pay as little as possible as late as they dare, and generally live with the constant strain of balancing on the brink of disaster.

When you're in denial, you reassure yourself that these are just temporary money problems that will disappear when you get your tax refund or your next raise—although the truth is that they've been going on for years, with no sign of abating. Unless a wise, caring partner helps you start perceiving reality on your own, it may take a real blast of cold air, like being dunned, sued, or refused a loan, to blow away this blinding fog.

Denial may be one of the biggest obstacles you'll face in trying to help an overspender confront his or her problem. If the spender values your respect, he or she won't be eager to admit this compulsion to you. And because like other addictive behaviors it provides fleeting moments of pleasure, he or she almost certainly won't be looking forward to giving it up. You can't simply say, "Okay, I know what's going on, and you better stop it!" Your partner will react with anger, resentment, and fear.

You'll need a great deal of tact and compassionate firmness to guide a reluctant partner into confronting the problem he or she has been denying. Try to present the problem in an objective way that asks for your partner's understanding and cooperation. Ideally, the spender then comes to view the agreed-to program as a win/win process instead of "you win/I lose." In the next chapter, when we talk about supportive communication, I'll offer some specific ideas you can use to help your partner break through the barrier of denial.

Defensiveness

Nobody likes feeling that he or she is to blame for conflict in a relationship. Thus, it's very common for people to react defensively by denying that they're at fault.

Defensiveness can be a particular obstacle if one partner's behavior is clearly more extreme than the other's. In an attempt to shift some of the responsibility to the more moderate partner, people may hide behind such face-saving defenses as "I'm not the only one who has problems here!" and "I'll change if you will."

Each of us must be honest enough to admit if we need more help in a particular area than our partner does. For example, if you're an out-of-balance spender and your hoarder partner is more balanced and rational, you must be willing to acknowledge that you have more to answer for if the conflict between you is to be resolved.

This doesn't mean the less-burdened partner should sit back and feel smug about his or her position. The best way to ensure that transformation will occur is for each person to take 100 percent responsibility for correcting his or her own imbalances. In fact, unless both of you are willing to help remedy what you helped create, there's no chance of turning around your relationship's destructive dynamics—as this example makes clear.

When Denial Meets Defensiveness: The Story of Felix and Evelyn

Evelyn and Felix's marriage had all the earmarks of a golden romance: after years of single life, they'd met when they served together on jury duty. On their wedding day, they were both in their mid-forties—happy testimony to the fact that love is not just for the young.

But now, with their first anniversary barely behind them, their marriage was in serious trouble, and they began therapy.

Evelyn was a hoarder who loved to save money. Before meeting Felix, she'd lived a very simple life for over twenty years, putting much of her salary into certificates of deposit, savings bonds, and other conservative investments. Since their marriage, she'd grown increasingly panicky. Felix, she said, was an out-of-control gambler who would end up running through her savings and leaving them both destitute in their old age.

Felix countered that the problem wasn't as extreme as Evelyn claimed. Although he'd borrowed nearly $18,000 this past year to pay gambling debts incurred at the casino and the racetrack, he felt he'd be able to repay the money easily when his luck began to turn.

Evelyn wanted Felix to stop gambling and let her manage his money. Felix wanted Evelyn to stop griping about his betting, since she wasn't willing to lend him the money to pay off his debts. In other words, each of them was insisting that he (or she) had no problem, that the other was at fault, and that things would be fine if only the other party would change.

Despite coaching in techniques of respectful communication, there just wasn't enough trust, openness, and goodwill in their relationship for either Felix or Evelyn to admit personal responsibility for their discord. With so much hurt and anger fueling their conflict, neither felt safe enough to move toward the middle.

Sadly, the fate of their relationship is unknown, since their therapy broke down soon after it began. Perhaps they eventually found the self-knowledge, compassion, and forgiveness they needed to work things out.

Secrecy

If you're in a relationship that is committed and ongoing, it's absolutely essential for each of you to have a good idea of the other's financial attitudes and feelings, as well as the finances themselves. In particular, you should be aware of any of these emotional issues that might be affecting your partner:

- Past traumas and fears concerning money

- Hopes and dreams

- Family money history, including successes, failures, disasters, achievements, and attitudes toward money communicated by relatives, teachers, or other key influences

When it comes to money facts and figures, I believe each partner has a right to know this information about the other:

- Income

- Debts

- Financial assets and liabilities

- Any past money crises of significance, such as a tendency to overdraw accounts or overload on debt; default on loans or bankruptcy

Part of the reason why so many people enter relationships with little knowledge of their partner's moneylife is that we tend to keep secrets from each other out of embarrassment, shame, or a deliberate desire to deceive.

Money secrets like compulsive overspending are particularly

hard to admit. Whether we're dating, living together, or married, most of us aren't resolute enough to confess that we have little or no control when it comes to spending money . . . and perhaps that we're also seriously in debt. If this truth got out, we fear, our partner would feel betrayed, lose respect for us, and maybe even end the relationship. Alas, the facts almost always come to light—try as we may to hide them—sometimes destroying trust that is difficult to regain, as this couple discovered.

Communication and financial problems brought Frank and Lila, his second wife, to my office.

A Matter of Trust: The Story of Lila and Frank

Frank was an overspender who felt he deserved lavish vacations, whether or not he had the money. While Lila might ordinarily have been glad to help him change his behavior, there was a serious obstacle: Frank had led her to believe he made much more money than he actually did. Furthermore, he'd never told her that he was still paying thousands of dollars for his two sons' college educations. As a result, he actually was able to contribute very little income.

Lila had grown up in a traditional family, where it was expected that the man of the house would be the chief provider. When she discovered that most of the expenses of their household were on her shoulders, not Frank's, she felt deceived, used, overwhelmed, and panicky. Though Frank would have risked losing her if he'd told her the truth early in their relationship, the fact that he had avoided telling her the whole story for so long only heightened her distrust and insecurity.

Frank and Lila have continued in therapy, working to repair the wounds created by his secrecy and her dashed expectations.

They've resolved how much each of them will contribute to the family income, and are helping each other to develop more empathetic communication skills. While rebuilding trust hasn't been a quick or easy process, they're working hard to heal their relationship.

In general, deliberate secrecy about money matters is a mistake. Like subterranean tensions building up along a fault line, the potential for devastation keeps growing as long as the secret is kept. When the great upheaval finally comes, it can tear apart the relationship.

Lying and Cheating

Money secrets—what might be called sins of omission—can be bad enough for a relationship, as the story of Frank and Lila shows; still worse are sins of commission—deliberate cheating or lying about money to one's partner. When this is uncovered, the innocent person's trust in his or her partner is apt to be completely shattered. Only self-confrontation and total honesty stand a chance of repairing the damage.

Your Cheatin' Heart: The Story of Herb and Denise

Newlyweds Denise and Herb were barely speaking to each other when they first sat down in my office. The cause of their rift was that Herb had "borrowed" $100 in birthday money that Denise had received from her parents and left in an envelope on her dresser. When she found out (just before he was about to tell her, he said), she felt outraged, betrayed, and unable to continue trusting him.

At the start of couples therapy, Herb seemed genuinely remorseful. Behind his recently erratic money behavior, he told us, were some serious problems caused by an incompetent securities broker he'd once used. As he began to open up more and more about himself, it seemed we were really making progress in repairing the bridge of trust between Denise and her husband.

Then, a few weeks into the therapy, Denise came to a session visibly shaken. Someone who'd called their home looking for Herb had told her Herb had once been caught accepting kickbacks from a vendor he'd encouraged his company to use. As it happened, Denise had also recently learned that Herb's problems with the investment brokerage were largely his own doing, contrary to the story he'd told us. Together, these two revelations completely destroyed her fragile sense of trust in him.

Their marriage dissolved shortly afterward. Again, Herb seemed truly devastated by this turn of events. He'd obviously feared that if he told Denise the truth about his money problems at the outset, she might have rejected him. It's also possible, of course, that she might have given him a chance to prove his trustworthiness. But between his deceiving her and his dishonesty in other areas, he'd lost any hope of earning the trust of a woman who'd loved him.

For many couples, spending money is the ultimate power play. If you feel powerless to obtain fulfillment of your deeper needs, either because you can't communicate them or because your partner won't respond with nurturing

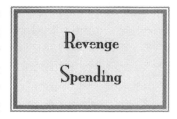

Revenge Spending

support, "revenge spending" is an all-too-common ploy. Usually, but not always, the spender is female—for example, a woman who suspects her spouse is having an affair, or a workaholic's wife who is fed up with being at the bottom of his priority list. Feeling aggrieved, abandoned, and betrayed, these women may go on a shopping binge to console themselves or deliver a sharp jab in the wallet to their absent spouse, or both.

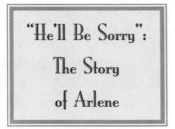

"He'll Be Sorry": The Story of Arlene

One of the most hair-raising tales of revenge spending I've ever heard was while I was a guest on a TV call-in show discussing money conflicts.

I never knew the caller's name, but let's call her Arlene. Arlene told us that she'd been disabled in a car accident some years before. Now unable to work, she was a virtual shut-in who cared for her aging mother at home. Her husband, she said, was a mean-spirited bully who made her beg for every penny she needed and doled out the money grudgingly, a bit at a time.

Speaking to me and the entire TV audience, Arlene announced that she was so furious with her stingy husband that she'd decided on an unusual (and definitely illegal) variation on revenge spending. What she'd done was set up a credit-card scam, first tricking people out of their credit-card numbers over the phone, then ordering merchandise for herself using these strangers' card numbers. If she was ever caught, she boasted, she'd arranged things so that her husband would take the rap.

As this brief phone call ended, I had a chilling sense that Arlene almost hoped this would happen. "He'll be sorry!" she concluded viciously—and hung up.

❧

These last obstacles to healing overspending—outright lying, cheating, and revenge spending—are extreme cases of highly negative behavior, of course. Most overspenders are much less malicious and less apt to be upset enough to retaliate out of rage, hurt, or spite. Even so, you may face considerable difficulty in encouraging a spender to confront his or her behavior. The likeliest barrier of all is this last one.

If your partner has a compulsive need to spend (or any other money compulsion, for that matter), he or she will find it almost impossible to reverse this destructive behavior singlehandedly. I've found that like alcoholism, compulsive spending seems to be an affliction that willpower alone can't overcome. Support groups such as Debtors Anonymous, friends, loving partners, and money mentors who can help when the spender is tempted to go on a binge can all be sources of tremendous support and healing.

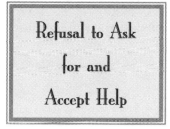

Refusal to Ask for and Accept Help

Refusal of this help may bring tragic results—loneliness, isolation, marital discord, even divorce. But many overspenders feel humiliated by the discovery that they have a problem they can't solve themselves. In our culture, men especially are taught to be self-sufficient, twenty-first-century cowboys who never met a problem they couldn't lick. Joining them on this precarious pedestal are their wives and sisters, schooled to consider themselves super-women capable of coping with anything and ashamed to seek help for a bad habit they mistakenly feel they could control with a little more willpower.

There's nothing shameful about seeking help, whether from a partner, a therapist, a friend, or a Debtors Anonymous group. We all need help sometimes to cope with the curveballs that life throws at us. That's why we exercise our bodies in aerobics or t'ai chi, and stretch our minds in continuing education; why we consult doctors and therapists to help us heal.

Willingness to ask for help is a sign of strength and courage, not of weakness or inadequacy. And as we'll see in the next chapter, by communicating in a way that makes the spender feel respected and appreciated, and less vulnerable and ashamed, a caring partner can help build a bridge of understanding and trust—the platform from which you both can determine what needs to be done to rebalance saving and spending in your relationship.

PART THREE

∽

Tools and Techniques You Both Can Use

7.

The ABCs of Supportive

Communication

I n the best of all possible worlds, you'd now be able to acknowledge to each other that one of you has become an overspender for reasons that may be very deeply rooted, that the other is involved too, and that you're committed to working together wholeheartedly to establish money harmony in your relationship. This candid communication would then continue as you progress together through the moneytalks that support the recovery process, allowing you to share thoughts, emotions, and suggestions freely.

In the real world, this open, earnest communication is complicated by the fact that over the years, compulsive spending has become entrenched in the spender's sense of self. In dropping the barriers of secrecy, shame, or denial that have kept this problem hidden from sight, the spender becomes vulnerable to being hurt—and in turn, gains the power to hurt a caring partner who may have simply hoped to help.

To resolve the problem, you have to learn what may be an en-

tirely new way of communicating openly, respectfully, and empathetically with each other. This supportive communication has its
own set of ABCs—rules that try to make sure you'll help, not hurt,
each other.

The 12 Secrets of Communicating Effectively

It seems as though we ought to know
how to communicate well without any
effort—after all, we've been jabbering
away to each other since infancy. But in
the moneytalks that are a key part of
healing, we need to communicate with
each other in a particularly intimate
way that builds bridges between hearts and minds.

For a spender trying to share the feelings surrounding binges,
communication is most effective when it's courageously vulnerable,
helping both you and your partner to understand the issues that
must be resolved for healing to occur. For a spender's partner, communication is truly effective when it's encouraging, compassionate,
firm when necessary, and equally vulnerable—a wish list of qualities that would challenge even the deftest diplomat.

To communicate in a way that works for both partners, it's
essential to follow these ground rules:

1. TRY A "WARM START" TO LAUNCH MORE OPEN COMMUNICATION

To encourage more vulnerable, even-handed sharing of information, I recommend you begin by accentuating the positive. For example, start a moneytalk by saying, "Here's what I really admire

about the way you are with money." No matter how out of balance you may feel your partner's behavior is, look carefully and you'll find something to admire—for example, the way he or she beautifies your home, finds memorable gifts for people, has fun when you both go on vacation, or spots a bargain. (If you truly can find nothing to appreciate about your partner's way with money, offer a positive comment about some other area in which he or she excels.)

2. STRESS THAT YOUR PARTNER'S ASSETS OUTWEIGH HIS OR HER FAULTS

Once you've started off with a warm-up, move on to share your fears and concerns about your partner's spending behavior. Do this as concisely as possible, with the goal of having the positive (what you appreciate) outweigh the negative (what concerns you). By beginning this way, you remind your partner that he or she still has your respect and affection.

3. KEEP IN MIND THAT NEITHER OF YOU IS PERFECT

In other words, be humble. Don't assume that the spender is the only one with a problem; each of you has shortcomings and biases that show up in the way you manage money (and in other areas as well). In fact, you'll both benefit by approaching each moneytalk with a sense of curiosity, vulnerability, and openness about your own money attitudes and behavior as well as your partner's.

4. TRY NOT TO BE ACCUSATORY OR JUDGMENTAL, AND USE "I" MESSAGES

Make a commitment to avoid blaming or abusive language, and practice respectful communication instead. One way to achieve this is to position your concerns in the context of your personal fears, anxieties, and other feelings, your own struggles with saving and spending, and the effect of your partner's behavior on you.

For example, tell your partner, "I feel afraid and helpless when you spend a lot of money without consulting me," instead of "Sometimes you act like an inconsiderate jerk!" This allows the other person to empathize with you and want to help solve the problem, instead of reacting to a stinging accusation with hostility and defensiveness.

In following this "I" principle, be careful not to use wolf-ish accusations in sheep's clothing, such as "I feel you have a serious spending problem" or "Your secret spending binges are driving me crazy!" Remember, your goal is not to wound, but to heal.

5. USE LANGUAGE THAT MAKES YOU ALLIES, NOT ENEMIES

Instead of shouting, "Give me your credit cards—I'm going to cut them up before you bankrupt us!", enlist your partner's help in your campaign against overspending. Solving the problem becomes a win/win effort for both of you when you phrase it like this:

"If we keep on spending so much, we won't be able to afford that vacation to Mexico we've been planning. I'm feeling frustrated and hopeless about what we could do to change this. Do you have any ideas?"

6. DON'T RUSH THE COMMUNICATION PROCESS

Take the time to make sure all thoughts and feelings are aired before moving toward negotiation or accord.

If talking about overspending is awkward or painful for you, you may be tempted to hurry through what you have to say: "I'm worried that we're spending too much. How about if we set some limit on our discretionary spending, like $40 a week? You don't have any problem with that, do you?" Or, if you're the spender, you may blurt out an angry response to your partner's attempt to convey concern: "Oh no, not this again! Are you going to lecture me? I don't want to hear about it!"

When either of you is tempted to ride roughshod over any objections ("Now here's what we're going to do . . ."), or to panic and overreact to a perceived slam ("You're always criticizing me!"), slow down. Remember that your partner needs to be sure of your respect and goodwill, and that your goal is to find a way where you both can win.

Take a deep breath. If you're really upset, "go away" for a moment, conjuring up a scene that makes you slow down inside. Some people visualize a serene ocean beach or woodsy glade. You might slow yourself down by imagining that the two of you are having a warm, heartfelt conversation, or remembering your most recent loving contact with your partner. Then, when you feel ready, return peacefully to your conversation.

7. BE OPEN AND VULNERABLE ABOUT YOUR MORE FRAGILE FEELINGS

Only by sharing your true emotions with each other can the two of you really understand and resolve the issues that fuel overspending. Although you may wish you could appear calm, confident, and in control, your partner will respond more freely if you express the fear, guilt, or anxiety you really feel. These feelings are important, so don't slight them by rushing through your comments.

This is a particularly important discipline for men to practice, since they tend to be less open and more abrupt in expressing their feelings. Try to share your emotions fully enough to give your partner time to adjust to what you're saying. For example, a spender's partner might say:

"Honey, I'm scared and worried about how much debt we have. I have trouble sleeping lately because I'm so concerned about this. I'd really like to work with you on figuring out some way to resolve this situation." After finishing, take a breath. If your partner doesn't volunteer a comment, ask, "How do you feel about this?" Finally, after receiving the spender's emotional feedback, you can suggest, "Is there something you'd be willing to do to help me with this?"

8. DON'T USE TRUSTINGLY CONFIDED INFORMATION AGAINST EACH OTHER

Before you and your partner begin what you hope will be honest, candid moneytalks, you need to agree that you won't use the information you learn as ammunition for future fights. If you do, your partner has the right to stop you in midsentence, remind you of your promise, and refuse to continue listening until you change track.

For example, if you learn that as a child your partner felt humiliated by having to live in a dilapidated house on the wrong side of the tracks, it's unfair to use this knowledge by protesting, "Don't take it out on me! I'm not forcing you to live in a shack, am I?" In finding the courage to share these painful memories with you, your partner trusts you to recognize that they are real wounds and to do what you can to help heal them.

It's okay to use this knowledge in a positive way. For example, you might say, "Honey, I know you grew up feeling ashamed of your family home and that you put up with a lot when we were just getting started and living in a trailer. I want you to feel happy and proud of the lovely home we have now. But I'm concerned that we're overspending in this area. Would you be willing to set a limit each month on the money you spend on home furnishings?"

9. GIVE YOUR PARTNER THE BENEFIT OF THE DOUBT

Assume the best about his or her motivations. A spender might say to a hoarder partner, "I understand that you feel responsible for making sure we can both retire comfortably. That's important to me too. But I feel anxious thinking that we won't be able to enjoy the good things of life now because we're so totally focused on the future." Mention some of the financial constraints that concern you and make space for your partner to share his or her needs and fears. Then you might propose, "Couldn't we work out a plan to satisfy both of these goals?"

Or a spender's partner might say, "I know you want our kids

to have the best of everything, and I do, too. I certainly don't want them to have to wear shabby clothes or go hungry, as you did when you were growing up. But I'm concerned that we're trying so hard not to deprive them that we're living beyond our means."

10. LISTEN WITH RESPECT AND EMPATHY

As you share feelings and memories about money and spending with each other, learn to listen with empathy. This means trying to put yourself in your partner's place and to walk a mile in his or her moccasins. For example, if you grew up in a relatively well-off family and never had to worry about whether you could afford college, try to imagine how different your viewpoint would be if you'd been brought up in your partner's single-parent family, existing on a precarious financial lifeline of child support, welfare, food stamps, and part-time work.

If you're a saver and not a spender, it may be especially hard for you to understand the torment spenders go through when they have to deny themselves something they want. This deprivation attack—what I call an inner tantrum—is a combination of intense rage, sadness, and emptiness, a painful emotion that hoarders simply don't experience under the same circumstances. In fact, when hoarders rein in a (rare) whim to spend, they tend to feel virtuous, balanced, and in control. If you're a hoarder by nature, you may find it difficult to empathize with the pain and deprivation spenders feel at having to say *no* to themselves.

11. USE EMPATHETIC PLAYBACK
TO ASSURE YOUR PARTNER THAT
YOU'RE REALLY LISTENING

Playback is a communication technique that helps your partner feel heard and understood. Inspired by the "verification and feedback channels" of clinical couples expert Isaiah Zimmerman and "mirroring" techniques taught to me by Harville Hendrix, it consists of clearly confirming what you think your partner has just said about some emotional topic.[1] You needn't repeat your partner's words verbatim, so long as you summarize the message in the spirit in which it was communicated. Then, ask whether you heard your partner as he or she wished to be heard.

If the answer is *no*, pay attention to your partner's clarification, then play back the revised message as reassurance that you've been listening carefully. If your partner agrees that you've heard accurately and in the right spirit, affirm your understanding with a comment like "That makes sense." And if you now appreciate your partner's emotional state more deeply, you might add an empathetic comment beginning with a phrase like "I imagine you might also be feeling . . . ," trying to sense nuances in your partner's feelings.

12. BE PATIENT IN DEALING
WITH DENIAL AND SHAME

If it's difficult for the spender to acknowledge that a problem exists, I recommend that his or her partner respectfully ask for some time to discuss an important matter. Then try to share in a vulnerable and compassionate way how the spender's behavior is affecting you.

When you state your concern in terms of how this behavior makes you feel, it becomes harder for the spender to persist in denial. If the going is tough, don't try to corner your partner into admitting there's a problem; instead, simply ask that he or she think about it and sit down with you to discuss it soon. Try to set a specific time you can get back together.

Shame is an equally touchy matter, apt to raise its head at any point during the recovery process. Remember that at times (particularly after a setback) the spender is apt to feel hypersensitive about his or her problem and may reject even the most kindly meant suggestion or comment. Swallow your impulse to insist, "It's for your own good!" Your partner knows that, but feels too vulnerable at the moment to accept your input.

Instead of continuing to press the matter, this might be a good time to mention some of your partner's positive qualities you love and appreciate. Or simply say, "I love you, honey" and, reminding yourself that you can talk together later, wait patiently until your partner is ready to open up to you again.

❧

Special Tips for Spenders' Partners

Be aware and appreciative of the spender's progress.
Avoid using words like "you're being good" in commenting on your partner's progress. That sends the message that you'll think a relapse makes him or her "bad."

To let your partner know how much you admire the efforts you've witnessed, you might say, for example, "When we were at the mall today, I noticed you went into your favorite store and came out again without buying anything. I want to tell you how hard I know that must be sometimes, and how much I appreciate your courage in working to change how you spend money. It makes me feel much closer to you."

Be tactful but firm if your partner has given in to temptation.

Don't scold, sigh in disappointment, or ignore the lapse. To help the spender want to get back on the track to recovery, you need to address the subject gently and sympathetically: "Honey, I know you had a relapse in spending this month. Setbacks like these are normal. Do you want to talk about it?" You might add, "Was there something going on emotionally when you had the urge to buy? Is there any way I can help you next time, or anything we could do together?"

Don't just "talk the talk" of being supportive; "walk the walk."

Let your spender partner know you're willing to go out of your way to help him or her follow through on the commitment to recover. For example, you might say, "I know it's hard to find the time and energy to go to a Debtors Anonymous or Shopaholics Ltd. meeting after work. But I also know these meetings give you the support you need to keep feeling better about yourself. I'll be glad to make dinner for us on your meeting nights, or do whatever else I can to help you get there."

To some extent, you'll be walking the tightrope between helping and overgiving. It's okay to make a special effort to jump-start your partner's recovery process, but over the long haul, he or she has to be the one who makes the program work. Once it's under way, you should be contributing way less than 50% of the effort to keep it moving.

Work on your own growth issues, and share your struggles.

If you're the hoarder (or milder spender) in the relationship, keep monitoring your own tendency to control, worry, tighten up, and deny yourself. To remind your partner that *both* of you are working toward money harmony, you might open up about your own struggles. For example, you might explain, "I know I tend to be an old tightwad, but please don't spend a lot of money on a birthday gift for me. I enjoy feeling loved and cared for more than anything else. If it will help, here are some ideas for inexpensive gifts I'd really appreciate, or things you could do which wouldn't cost anything." You might add empathetically, "I know this may take some of the pleasure out of gift-giving for you, and I'm truly sorry about that—but I would really feel great if you could do this for me."

Seven Communication No-Nos for Caring Partners

Some of the following negative tactics may seem to work in the heat of the moment. Over time, however, they'll create resentment and may generate hidden paybacks—either in secret overspending, or in other behavior that undermines your relationship.

1. *No angry explosions.* Don't attack in anger and exasperation with outbursts like "I can't believe you spent this much on that old beat-up deacon's bench!"

2. *No scare tactics.* Threats of imminent disaster usually don't work. "If you keep this up, we're going to go bankrupt/I'm going to have a nervous breakdown/you're going to end up a bag lady!" If scare tactics like these were effective, every cigarette smoker in the world would have quit years ago.

3. *No threats or ultimatums.* You may feel frustrated enough to vow, "If you don't stop this, I'm going to move out!"—but don't say it. Your partner already feels helpless enough against his or her compulsion. A threat like this simply adds more feelings of guilt and despair to an already crushing burden.

4. *No nasty accusations.* A quick way to derail your dialogue is to start calling each other names: "If you'd stop acting like a spoiled brat . . ." "Why are you such an old cheapskate?"

5. *No guilt trips or sweeping criticisms.* Don't take an occasional oversight or a modest flaw and blow it up into earthshaking proportions. For example: "You're always thinking of yourself! When are you going to start paying some attention to me and the kids for a change?"

6. *No parental platitudes.* Try not to sound like your father or mother—or worse. "Do you think money grows on trees?" is patronizing enough. "Look, I'll try to say this simply enough for you to understand" is infuriating.

7. *No one-upmanship.* Maybe this should be called "one-*down*-manship," since it consists of trading low blows verbally with your partner. A sample of this destructive dialogue might be:

"We'd be okay if you weren't so weird about money!"

"*Me* weird? You're the one who . . ."

"Well, I wouldn't have done that if you hadn't . . ."

"Everything's *my* fault, isn't it? You don't care what I'm going through!"

"You don't care much what I'm going through, either, or you
wouldn't be so hostile all the time!"
"*You're* the one who's hostile!"

A Demonstration Dialogue

To give you an idea how good communication principles can help you and
your partner start a healthy, mutually
respectful conversation, here's an example of dialogue that moves from denial toward agreement and action:

PARTNER: Honey, I need to talk to you about something important.
Would now be a good time?

SPENDER: Oh—now is fine, I guess. What is it?

PARTNER: You know, I think your taste is wonderful—you've filled
our home with so many beautiful things. But I'm starting to
dread sitting down with our bills each month. The amount of
money we've been spending lately really worries me.

SPENDER: Well . . . I guess I've been buying a lot of stuff lately, but
I didn't think it was that serious.

PARTNER: I wish we could buy everything we want, but I'm afraid
we need to start setting some priorities. If we keep on spending
more than we make, we actually might have to declare bankruptcy.

SPENDER: You're calling it "our" spending, but it's me you're talking about, isn't it? I wish you would get off my back about
spending money! The Joneses make almost exactly as much as
we do, and they just bought a new Anaconda Luxor with the
deluxe George Hamilton interior package. I think my spending
is really pretty reasonable by comparison!

PARTNER: I'm sorry if I've come across as angry and impatient. I don't mean to. But I'm afraid that if we don't do something, our credit will be ruined for years and we won't be able to buy a home as we planned. Is there anything I can do to help you get your spending under control?

SPENDER: Listen, I've tried before. I'm hopeless.

PARTNER: I notice you seem to shop more when I'm out of town. Is there something I could do to help you there?

SPENDER: How about telling your boss you won't travel anymore?

PARTNER: I wish I could. But maybe sometimes you could come with me. Or if you can't, what if I call you more often?

SPENDER: Are you really serious? I'm impressed! It's so nice to hear you care about the way I feel. . . . Sometimes I can stay busy and hardly notice you're gone. Other times I start missing you when you walk out the door, and all day long I think about the interesting things you're doing. It makes me feel kind of low, and that's when I really want to get out of the house. So I go shopping.

PARTNER: One of the things I'm hearing you say is that being busy helps you keep from feeling lonely or bored and wanting to go out shopping. Did I understand you?

SPENDER: Yes, I do get lonely. And maybe I'm a little jealous that I'm stuck at home without anything to do.

PARTNER: Hmm, yeah. I can understand that.

SPENDER: Maybe I should consider looking for a job. But I don't know . . . it's a big step.

PARTNER: I know, it would be a major change for you. But I think finding work you enjoy would make you happy. Don't you?

SPENDER: I'm just a little scared. It's been so long since I had a job. . . . I guess I'm not really sure how to get started.

PARTNER: I'd be glad to help you with a resumé. You've got a lot of talents. I think any company would be lucky to hire you!

SPENDER: You don't suppose you might be a little prejudiced?

PARTNER: Who, me? No way! *(They both laugh.)*

SPENDER: Let's talk about it some more when you get home tonight.
PARTNER: It's a deal.

> ## Take Time to Learn the Language of Healing

Don't be upset or angry with yourself if it takes longer than you'd thought to master the ABCs of supportive communication. While you're learning, recognize that you'll stumble now and then and say something that may cause hurt, anger, guilt, or resentment in your partner.

When this happens, ask your partner to let you know instead of brooding about it or flaring up. Don't be too proud to apologize; sincere regrets can go a long way toward building a more trusting relationship. And try to react with a similar openness when it happens to you.

8.

Working It Out Together

If a lack of past openness or goodwill makes the two of you feel a little awkward talking in a vulnerable way to each other, here are five excellent exercises to encourage closer communication.

I developed this exercise to help couples learn to give each other what they want and need in everyday conversation. It's something you can do together once a day, once a week, or whenever you want.

The Perfect
Conversation

To initiate the perfect conversation, start by telling your partner the subject you're going to talk about (for example, the kind of day or week you had, or how your client presentation went), and ask him or her to respond in a specific way.

For example, you might say, "I'm going to talk about my day

today, and I want you to smile and look friendly. When I talk about accomplishments, I want you to look me in the eye and say, 'That's great,' and when I talk about disappointments or frustrations, I want you to say, 'That's terrible.' "

Then you go ahead and share whatever you want to about your day, while your partner tries to give you the kind of responsiveness you asked for. At the end, let your partner know what you particularly appreciated about his or her responses. Your comments must all be positive and supportive; no negative feedback is allowed.

Then the two of you switch roles, so you're now the listener complying with your partner's rules for the perfect conversation. Couples who have tended to tune each other out over the years will find that this exercise improves their ability to meet each other's real needs by listening and responding to one another in satisfying conversation.

Reromanticizing the Relationship

Remember how it felt when the two of you first fell in love? In this exercise (adapted from a therapy suggested by Harville Hendrix[1]), I want each of you to list things that make you feel loved. Divide your lists into three parts:

* What your partner used to do in your "honeymoon phase" to make you feel loved.

* What he or she does now to make you feel loved and appreciated.

* What your partner could do to make you feel loved that he or she has never done before.

Exchange your lists and discuss them. During this discussion, each of you should communicate which items from your partner's list you'd be willing to do, which ones you would not be willing or able to do, and which ones you'll think about doing. Then, each of you should try to practice one idea a day from this list until these habits become integrated into your life, enriching and reromanticizing your relationship.

If you feel as though you and your partner are like two trains traveling on different tracks, sometimes passing each other but seldom on the same schedule, this exercise developed by Christopher Mogil and Anne Slepian of The Impact Project can help.[2]

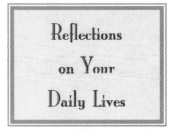

Reflections on Your Daily Lives

Set aside fifteen minutes toward the end of each day to share this information with one another:

* *Highlights:* Tell about two things you enjoyed today.

* *Accomplishments:* Share two things you're proud of having done today.

* *Challenges:* Talk about one thing that was hard for you, and what lesson you've learned from it.

* *Action:* Describe one action you'd like to take in the coming week to increase the impact of any of these highlights, achievements, or lessons in your life.

Structured communications like these can strengthen intimacy between a couple who have been finding it hard to take the time to connect regularly.

> **Love Letters to Your Partner**

Ironically, this exercise can be most helpful when you're not feeling particularly loving because something has blocked you from communicating openly with your partner.

The subject matter can be anything you're hesitant to sit down and discuss with your partner. A shy spender, for example, might write a love letter if his or her partner has been trying to control instead of help. A spender's discouraged partner might write a love letter if the spender has jeopardized their financial situation by exceeding prearranged spending limits.

As created by John Gray (author of *Men Are From Mars, Women Are From Venus*)[3], an effective love letter moves from negative to positive feelings in a way that can illuminate and dissolve the obstacle blocking your communication with your partner. It always has five sections:

1. *Anger.* What did your partner do to make you feel mad, hurt, or frustrated?

2. *Sadness.* What did he or she do to disappoint you?

3. *Fear.* What did he or she do to make you worried or anxious?

4. *Regret.* What do you wish had happened differently? What are you embarrassed about, ashamed of, or remorseful for? How would you repair the damage?

5. *Love.* What do you appreciate about your partner? What positive wishes and impulses would you express? How would you tell your partner of your love?

Give yourself some privacy and quiet to write your love letter. As you work on it, imagine your partner reading it with love and understanding. Try to express your feelings simply and briefly, using "I feel" statements to communicate your point of view without accusing or judging your partner.

When you're done, write your partner's response to this love letter. You may put in it the exact words you'd like to hear. Or, to work toward more insight into your partner's point of view, you might follow the same five steps you pursued in writing your own letter.

For example, a spender feeling overcontrolled by her spouse might write:

Dear Nick,

I feel angry that you put our tax refund into a CD without consulting me.

I am disappointed that you didn't trust me enough to let me join you in deciding what to do with our money.

I worry that if you refuse to let me participate in managing our money, I will never have the self-confidence to stand on my own two feet, or feel that we are a real team.

I wish you'd given me the chance to prove to you and to myself that I can make sensible money decisions.

I love you. I respect your strength and knowledge, and want to become the kind of partner you can respect and rely on in everything.

Love, Nora

Here's the "perfect response" letter Nora then wrote:

Dear Nora,

I feel upset that it's so much easier for you to spend money than to save it, although I know you are working to remedy this.

I'm sad that my decision to put the refund money into a CD caused so much tension and unhappiness between us.

I worry that unless we start saving more money, I will not be able to support you and look after you as I want to.

I'm sorry I was so thoughtless in investing that money without consulting you. I didn't mean to hurt your feelings—I was hurrying and forgot that this was your money too.

I love you and admire you for being willing to change spending habits you've had for years. I'll try to work harder on giving you an equal share of the financial responsibility.

Love, Nick

After you've finished both the original love letter and the "perfect response," it's up to you whether to show either or both of them to your partner. The exercise of expressing your feelings in these letters may make you feel so much better—more liberated, and more loving—that you don't have a communication block anymore.

Walk in Each Other's Shoes

This simple exercise can be tremendously powerful in teaching hoarder and spender partners to understand and empathize with each other's viewpoint.

Your mission: to set aside half an hour or forty-five minutes for a trip to your favorite store, during which you're going to trade roles. The spender partner gets to decide what you're going to "shop" for. If possible, it should be a big-ticket item, or at least something you wouldn't normally pay for out of pocket money (for example, a dining-room table, an easy chair, or a new TV). And it should be something you really need or could use.

When you enter the store, switch roles. If you're normally the hoarder of the couple, for the duration of this shopping trip I want you to pretend you're an eager spender like your partner. The spender, in turn, must play the role of his or her hoarder partner, focused on spending as little as possible.

Listen to each other as you shop—and when your time is up, sit down, resume your normal roles, and compare notes. I promise you'll have a much deeper understanding of your partner's approach to money and from then on will be able to communicate much more openly with your equally enlightened partner.

Not long ago, I found myself in a situation where the power of this role-reversal exercise became extraordinarily clear. To illustrate what empathy, open communication, and a joint commitment to changing money habits can accomplish, here is the exhilarating story of Mark and Rosemary.

Mark and Rosemary were engaged to be married when I met them. As meetings go, this one was rather public, taking place in front of several million viewers who were watching us on ABC-TV's "20/20". The show's producers had asked me to try to help this young couple, who were having serious spender/hoarder conflicts about money.

An Amazing Turnaround: The Story of Mark and Rosemary

Whenever Mark wandered into a department store, he behaved as if he were in a trance. Like a kid in a toy store, he wanted almost everything he saw, and he bought without giving any heed to whether or not he could afford it.

Rosemary, on the other hand, was so frugal that she'd lived for three years without a stick of furniture in her living room, saving every penny to make sure she'd never go hungry or be unable to pay her bills.

Watching this couple on video before I met them, I saw them argue in department stores (he wanted to buy this and that; she didn't want to buy anything) and in restaurants (he wanted the most expensive entrée; she wanted the blue-plate special, although it wasn't something she particularly liked). I was then invited to interview them on the air, teach them some money-therapy techniques, and take them shopping again.

In the interview, Rosemary confided childhood memories of being humiliated that her family had had to go on welfare after her father lost his job, and her determination never again to feel such agony as an adult. Mark recalled his upbringing as one of four children of a loving single mom, who worked at a pink-collar job and was always in debt. His description of her as "living on the edge and never seeming to notice it" fit Mark himself to a tee.

These two terrific people now loved and supported each other in almost every aspect of their life together. In a sort of trial by fire, they'd bravely decided to merge their finances *before* marriage to see if they could overcome the contrast in their moneystyles.

It wasn't working. In fact, the panic Rosemary felt at Mark spending "her" money and the frustration Mark felt at Rosemary hoarding "his" money were putting a severe strain on their relationship.

I gave them a challenging assignment. We three would go to Macy's to look at videocassette recorders and couches—two items Rosemary hadn't yet felt affluent enough to purchase. Rosemary's assignment would be to role-play being a spender like Mark, and he would role-play being a hoarder like his fiancée. The goal wasn't to buy something that day, but just to experience being in each other's shoes for a while. I coached each of them in their roles, and then we set off with the "20/20" camera crew for our forty-five-minute shopping trip.

The experience transformed them both. Rosemary walked around in an escalating frenzy, wanting to buy everything she saw: makeup, a compact disc player, the most expensive VCR with every conceivable feature, and so on. Mark kept saying things like "We're not buying this today. We have to go home and see whether we can afford this when we check our budget. Why are you looking at CD players and makeup? We agreed to stick to living-room couches and VCRs!"

When they'd finished their role-playing, they sat down right there at Macy's on a living-room couch they both liked (and which they'd decided they could afford after their next paycheck). I asked them to share their reactions to walking a mile in each other's shoes.

Mark was absolutely thunderstruck. Awed by his new awareness, he said, "No wonder she worries about money so much; I refuse to stick to any limits at all. I can't believe it—I'm really an addict!"

Rosemary said with a dazed smile, "No wonder he loves it so much! It's really seductive, shopping like that. It's like a chemical high."

After that experience, I encouraged them to seek ongoing money therapy to continue the progress they'd made. They also agreed to let Mark begin taking more responsibility in managing his money. I suggested that Mark might also want to join Debtors Anonymous for ongoing support.

Six months later, "20/20" interviewed this young couple again. Mark and Rosemary reported that they didn't fight about money anymore—in fact, the difference between now and then, they said, was like day and night. With their money harmony so vastly improved, they'd decided to go ahead with their wedding plans.

After this update aired, I called to ask them for more details of their progress. Exactly how had they managed to rebalance their money habits? Had they pursued the follow-up program we'd discussed?

Mark said he hadn't joined Debtors Anonymous, but he and Rosemary had been able to help each other transform their behavior. Rosemary added that they'd used my book *Money Harmony* "like a Bible," working on a chapter every week or two, including all the suggested exercises.

"So what happened?" I asked.

Mark sounded pleased and confident as he talked about the deep changes in his behavior. After discussing with me how to move toward money harmony, reflecting on what he'd unconsciously learned during his upbringing, and seeing his spending through Rosemary's eyes in that fateful shopping trip to Macy's, he'd begun to reduce his spending and now had much more self-control. "When we go shopping, I don't feel as though I have to buy something," he said. "Rose and I were in Macy's the other day, and she found a couple of sweaters she thought would look great on me. I looked them over, carried them around for a while, thought about them and about our other expenses, and finally said, 'I really don't need them,' and put them back. That *never* would have been possible before."

I congratulated Mark on the way he'd been able to translate his new awareness into healthier actions. He added, "I've realized something else about my shopping behavior. Whenever Rose and I were in a store and she ended up with something, I'd feel jealous and envious, like I had to buy something, too, or I'd be cheated. Now I don't feel deprived if we buy her something—I feel okay."

I was impressed by the calm and perceptive way Mark explained all this, and I found the details of his transformation extremely moving. He had changed in three important ways, he told me: "First, I began to see things from Rose's perspective. I saw what my overspending had done to her, why she'd cry at night and have nightmares about being put out on the street. Second, I became more aware of the way I thought about money and treated it, and I realized what was compulsive about my behavior.

"Third, I've gotten much more involved in our finances. I know how much money we have in our accounts now, and it's nowhere near as much as I used to think we had. With what we make and the bills we have to pay, we can't afford to shop a lot and eat out all the time. Rose and I sit down at least once a week to discuss our bills and decide what's needed to pay each one. If we have a real large payment due, I'll call the creditor and work out a payment plan we can handle." He paused, and then added appreciatively, "For the first time in my life, I feel in control of my money!"

I shared some details of my own spending recovery with Mark, noting how it can be particularly difficult around birthdays not to regress and want to spend money "treating" oneself. Mark knew exactly where I was coming from. "I used to go out and spend six or seven hundred dollars at a clip around my birthday," he admitted. "Now, with the holidays coming up, I actually found myself saying to Rose, 'I really don't need anything for Christmas. I'm getting the love and attention I need, and gifts seem unimportant. I can't believe I'm saying this, but I really mean it!' "

Mark's transformation was extraordinary. He really was living in a different world than the compulsive shopaholic one that had limited his horizons before. All these changes had clearly increased his self-esteem and given him a sense of involvement as well as autonomy—the combination of independence and interdependence integral to a couple's strength and harmony.

Next, I interviewed Rosemary. With evident delight, she told me she was now able to treat herself to a few simple pleasures now and then without feeling guilty. Mark's control of his spending habits had released her to "move toward the middle" in her own behavior.

I asked her, as I'd asked Mark, just what happened to make that possible. Rosemary said simply, "We separated our money. We each have our own checking account and our own set of credit cards. That one step took away 80 percent of the stress we used to have about money."

She went on to say, "That role reversal at Macy's was the best thing that ever happened to us. Now Mark really thinks before he buys. He asks himself, 'Do I really need this?' and often the answer is *no*." I could hear the smile in her voice. "He's also more open to learning from me, but I have to be careful how I come across. I used to lecture a lot: 'Do this—do that.' Now I just try to let him know the facts as I understand them, and let him decide how he wants to work it out."

Rosemary went on happily, "Mark balances his own checkbook. And he pays bills now! It's so cool. He pays the utilities and the phone bills. Then, slowly, he takes on two more bills. It's gradual, but it's working real well. He's actually fanatical about paying things off at the end of the month."

Obviously, Rosemary had learned to step back and give Mark enough space to do things his way. They'd both progressed—she from acting like a limit-setting parent and Mark from acting like a rebellious child—into a relationship of equals based on mutual respect, love, and acknowledgement of each other's strengths and weaknesses.

"I don't wake up in the middle of the night anymore and think about being a bag lady sleeping on a subway grating," Rosemary concluded. "We're having a lot of fun planning our wedding, and we've already decided how much we're going to spend on it. Life is great!'"

I certainly couldn't add anything to that conclusion. If you and your partner are as polarized in your moneylives as Rosemary and Mark were, take heart. With a combination of hard work, persistence, and love, this dedicated couple were able to turn their classic money conflict into a real success story.

PART FOUR

How Overspenders Can

Overcome

9.

Turning Your Overspending Around

N ow you are ready to grapple with the overspending that has
been ravaging your relationship. In this chapter, you'll find
ways to bring it out into the light of day, to recognize where
it may have sprung from, and to begin loosening its grip on you.

Before you begin this part of the program, I'd like you each to
buy a notebook (it can be the inexpensive kind kids use for school,
or as fancy as you wish). Use it regularly as a private journal to
record thoughts, feelings, and ideas about your money behavior,
and as a homework book to complete the written exercises in the
next few chapters. It's *your* money notebook—so feel free to scrib-
ble in it, diagram a spending binge . . . whatever you want.

The weapons I find most helpful
in changing people's attitudes
toward money are exercises that
ask the spender (and often the
partner) to probe deeply into feelings about money issues. These ex-
ercises usually serve as the focus of moneytalks—candid discussions

Finding Out What You're Dealing With

between the spender and his or her partner and/or a therapist.

In my couples therapy, I often use six awareness exercises that can be very helpful to both of you. I'll outline them on the assumption that you're both participating in this recovery program, since the best results tend to come when both partners work toward money harmony together—one of you learning to come to grips with your overspending and coping with it, the other one providing caring support and working on imbalances of his or her own (money-related or not). Try to keep your program moving steadily by regularly scheduling an hour or so of private time to work on it together. Find the pace that's best for you. Once a week may be plenty; more frequent sessions may burn you both out. Also, you need to allow enough time between sessions to think through what you've learned from the last money-talk and to prepare for the next one.

There's no rule that you have to chug along, covering one exercise in each moneytalk. In fact, some of these exercises may prove complex and interesting enough to be the subject of several discussions. In my therapy practice, we work with a particular exercise as long as it seems to be producing fresh insights, then decide (together) to move on.

We all know that the subject matter is serious. But as you'll see, these exercises aren't tiresome or difficult. In fact, some of them may be downright fun. I'll be glad if you think so—laughter is often especially healing.

Exercise 1: Share Your Money Feelings and Histories

Is your money behavior influenced by an inner child who was deprived, overindulged, or wounded long ago?

When I work with compulsive overspenders, one of the first things I do is ask how money was used and viewed in their family while they were growing up, along with their feelings about it.

Either partner can initiate this as the first awareness exercise, perhaps with an invitation that reminds you both of the rules of respectful communication: "I know we've had a lot of disagreements about money, and I'm partly responsible for them. It might help us to share how we feel about money. I'd be willing to tell you about my family history with money, if you'll do the same. I promise not to use what you tell me against you in future discussions. Are you willing to try it?"

For this exercise, I suggest you plan on two moneytalks, each lasting half an hour to an hour. If one of you feels vulnerable being the only partner "on stage," you may want to schedule both moneytalks in the same session (perhaps with a short breather between). Or you might choose to limit each session to just one person's perspective and schedule them on two consecutive days. This allows the designated listener to devote complete and respectful attention to the partner who's sharing information, without being distracted by thoughts of his or her own story.

Try to prepare for these moneytalks by thinking about the assignment and jotting down your feelings and memories. When you get together, you should be ready to share this kind of information:

* Your earliest memory about money.

* Who spent it, and on what; and how people in your family reacted to this behavior.

* Who saved money, and what for; and how people reacted to this behavior.

* Your family's money fears, messages, philosophy, habits.

* What you remember about family money fights and money tensions.

⚖ What you remember about the money you needed as a child, and what you did with it if you got it. Did you get a regular allowance? Was it ever withheld as punishment?

⚖ Any special thing you really wanted and got (or didn't get), and how you reacted to this.

⚖ Any other emotional memories about money and spending from your growing-up years, from inside or outside the family.

Remember, it's okay for the listener to be curious and ask interested questions. But respect your partner's vulnerability and make your questions understanding and encouraging, not critical or condescending.

Exercise 2: Share a Financial Status Report

If you aren't already acquainted with the details of each other's financial situation, this should be the topic for another early set of moneytalks—one for each of you. Or if your money is merged, the partner who has been making most of the decisions and paying the bills should prepare a report for both of you to discuss. I suggest you look at your money two ways:

YOUR NET WORTH

If you had to cash in everything you own and pay everything you owe right now, what would you have left? First add up your assets, including the estimated current market value of property like a house, car(s), furniture and other possessions, any savings or investments, and the cash value of any life insurance. Then subtract your liabilities, such as the principal you haven't yet paid off on a mortgage and other loans, outstanding credit-card or credit-line balances, and any other obligations. Whatever's left over is your net worth. (Yes, it may be a negative number. If it is, don't come unstrung. Nobody's asking you to cash in your chips just yet!)

YOUR CASH FLOW

During a typical month, where does your money go? First, list all sources of regular income: wages (before tax), freelance fees, income from rental property, etc. Then, subtract a typical month's expenses: your mortgage or rent, payments on car loans, student loans, or other installment debt; alimony or child support; average monthly credit-card or credit-line payments; transportation; groceries; clothing; health insurance; medical bills; Federal, state, and local income tax; Social Security and Medicare contributions; a month's worth of annual or quarterly expenses like property tax and premiums for home, car, life, or disability insurance; and so on. In a third category, show your monthly contributions to savings or a retirement plan.

The idea is that your total income should at least roughly equal your total expenses and savings contributions. If your expenses are significantly higher than your income and your savings are zilch, you have what accountants call a negative cash flow. (They usually look very grave when they say this, and ask you to pay them in cash instead of writing a check, "if you don't mind.")

In layman's terms, negative cash flow simply means that you're spending more money than you make. If this is the case, don't panic. You're in the same boat with a lot of other couples. Your next step should be to devote some time to identifying where expenses could be reduced to bring your cash flow back into balance. Because you're already concerned about overspending, it's likely that you'll find a lot of money has drained into discretionary categories such as clothing, entertainment, home furnishings, or gifts. Explore whether your partner is willing to join you in setting spending limits in these categories.

Have your bills reached the totally unmanageable high-tide line? Try to work out a reasonable repayment plan with your creditors. (Your nearest Consumer Credit Counseling Service office offers free help with a plan like this. See chapter 10.)

Note: If you've been faithfully copying data on deposits and withdrawals from your checkbook into a computer program like Quicken, you can print out a fairly useful cash flow report in a jiffy. (Someday, software like this will actually be *in* our checkbooks, and then none of us will have an excuse for not knowing that 7.328 percent of our gross monthly income goes for takeout dinners.)

Exercise 3: Keep Track of Your Expenditures and How You Feel When You Spend Money

The next thing I generally do with spender clients is invite them to keep track of what they buy and how much they spend for an entire week, down to the smallest purchase or payment.

This can be an extraordinarily valuable exercise for an overspender. If you'd prefer to keep your money notebook at home, buy another one that's small enough to tuck in your purse or pocket. Make sure it's formatted horizontally, like a book (not vertically, like a steno pad), because you'll be using left-hand pages to write down facts and figures, and right-hand pages to write down your feelings about any of those purchases that weren't routine or planned.

For example, let's say you're on your way home from work with a ho-hum evening ahead of you. On an impulse, you detour to the mall, remembering a sale ad for your favorite brand of shoes that appeared in the morning newspaper. You walk into the store, see a style you like, it fits, and you want to buy it.

What this exercise asks you to do is to stop for a moment anytime between your first impulse to go shopping and the actual purchase and pull out your little notebook. On the top half of a left-hand page, write down what you're thinking of buying ("Pair of dress shoes"), approximately what it will cost ("$35–$50"), and at what time or under what circumstances the idea first came to you ("About 5:40 P.M., on way home from office").

Directly opposite, on the top part of the right-hand page, jot down your feelings about this intended purchase: your emotions when you first thought of buying it ("Bored—wanted something interesting to do"), why you want the item ("Feel outdated/frumpy at office" or maybe "Want to impress sharp new client"), and how you think buying it would make you feel ("Happy—anticipate looking more sophisticated & successful to coworkers & boss" or perhaps "Will feel braver about asking new Asst. VP for date"). Take a moment more to write down how you'd feel if you *didn't* buy the item ("Let down, deprived, angry").

Try to make these entries in your notebook before you get out of your car or before you enter the store—if for no other reason than that you may feel a little self-conscious madly scribbling notes in front of a rack of pumps or wingtips.

Now let's say you go ahead and make your purchase. When you're back in the car, or when you get home, take out your notebook again, and on the bottom half of the same left-hand page write down the actual price and how you paid for the item

("$47.88, MasterCard"). Directly opposite, on the bottom half of the right-hand page, write your actual feelings after you made the purchase. (Also include how many hours you had to work to pay for it.) It's vital to be absolutely honest with yourself. If you feel upset or frustrated by your behavior, say so.

When you review your spending notes at the end of the week, you'll have a snapshot of your behavior that reveals quite a bit of information:

- How much money you spent.

- How much of it you spent on regular routine purchases (like groceries or gas) versus unplanned impulse buys.

- How much money you actually ended up spending on an impulse item, compared to what your "before" notes show you thought it might cost.

- What feelings or situations tended to trigger your desire to buy on impulse.

- How you felt afterward, compared to how you imagined you were going to feel.

- Whether the work time you had to put in to pay for each item was worth the price in terms of the pleasure it gave you.

Often a spending binge is so impulsive that clients can't or won't slow down enough to write down their feelings before they spend the money. Then, when they remember to note their thoughts and emotions after the episode is over, they tend to agonize in outpourings of self-hate, shame, and guilt for having splurged again. Though these "after" remarks underline how short-lived the pleasure of compulsive overspending is, the "before" comments can be even more helpful in identifying the deeper feelings that trigger your binges in the first place.

As you flip through the notebook at week's end, do you find that purchase after purchase starts off with feelings of loneliness at having nothing else to do after work? Or with frustration about your job or about a relationship you're in? Or with boredom, because you have too much empty time on your hands? Or with a desire to avoid family worries waiting for you at home? Unless these needs and feelings are unearthed, explored, and resolved, your shopping binges will almost certainly continue.

As you get used to recording your daily expenditures, I suggest you continue this process for an entire month to be sure your spending patterns emerge clearly. After the first week, it may be sufficient just to record dollar amounts and item descriptions— except for impulse purchases, which you should continue to report in detail.

Next, I'd like both of you to spend some time writing down (or tape-recording, if that's easier) a money dialogue. This is an imagined conversation between you and Money, discussing how your relationship with him/her/it is going. If you're a spender, focus on the spending aspect of your money behavior.

Exercise 4:
Imagine a
Conversation
with Money

As you work on this dialogue, consider questions like these:

* What kind of personality does Money have? For example, is it seductive, dictatorial, friendly, hostile, uncaring, pleasant . . . ?

* What does Money think of the way you've treated him/her/it?

* What's your justification for treating Money this way?

* What could you do to move your relationship with Money toward greater harmony?

Your money dialogue can be as short or as long as it takes to express your feelings. If the first draft accurately reflects your attitudes, don't spend a lot of time reworking it—you may only water it down.

When you've finished it, I'd like you to imagine the kind of comments you'd hear on this money dialogue from three authority figures in your past or present life—your mother, your father, and your Higher Power (God or your own inner wisdom). You may also "invite" the imagined comments of other people who have been powerful influences on the way you treat Money, such as your partner, a brother or sister, your best friend from school, an ex-spouse, or even Sister Mary Angelica who taught third-grade catechism class.

If your moneytalks so far have been successful, I would recommend that you and your partner set another date to share your money dialogue and this commentary. By helping to reveal your beliefs and some of their sources, this exercise can provide some hope and reinforcement in the difficult process of moving toward money harmony.

Here's how a sample dialogue might look. (The spender here happens to be female, but it could just as easily be a man.)

A SPENDER'S MONEY DIALOGUE

MONEY: You scatter me around and get rid of me so fast, I feel like a leper! What's your problem? Why can't you ever hold onto me, and feed and nourish me?

ME: There's always so many things I want—things to keep me happy, looking good, in step with my friends and with others at work . . .

MONEY: No matter how many "things" you buy, you still act like you don't really have what you want. Do you really need to have a new dress every other week, and new books or CDs every time you pass a bookstore or music store?

ME: It's not that I need them, but I want them so much. Why shouldn't I have them? My parents never said *no* to me, and I work hard, so why should I have to say *no* to myself? I want to enjoy life and let the future take care of itself. Or let my husband take care of it—he saves practically every penny he makes!

MONEY: Quite a bargain you've struck with him: He saves, you spend. Does that really sound fair to you? Personally, I think it stinks! And you pay for it with money fights and less and less lovemaking. Fess up. Your "deal" isn't working.

ME: Maybe you're right . . . but I can't stand the idea of giving up the things I want!

Commentary

MOTHER: You should have married a wealthier man who can give you everything you want. I never had to do without, and neither should you.

FATHER: My little girl deserves to have the best of everything. Just be happy, enjoy yourself! Your husband and I will look after the future for you.

BROTHER: You were always a spoiled brat, and you still are! I bet you won't be able to keep this up forever—and I'll be glad to see how you handle having to give up things, like the rest of us!

HUSBAND: You have all the fun, I have all the worry. It's not fair, and it just can't go on like this! Please look at yourself, honey, and look at the tug of war we've gotten ourselves into. Can't you try to meet me halfway? Otherwise, I don't know how all this will end, but I know it won't bring us love and happiness together.

HIGHER POWER: It makes me sad that you equate having "things" with being happy. You need to learn more about real happiness and fulfillment—but I'm afraid you never will, if you keep stuffing yourself with possessions and avoid looking deeper for true sources of nourishment. If you're willing to look at this, you'll have all the help you need from me and many others who love and support you.

A HOARDER'S MONEY DIALOGUE

MONEY: You're squeezing me so tight to your chest, I can't breathe! You know, I'm also meant to be used for things that would bring you and your family pleasure. What's going on with you?

ME: I'm just so scared you won't be around when I'm older, I don't dare let you go now. If I did buy expensive gifts for myself or anyone else, I'd feel wasteful and self-indulgent.

MONEY: Sure, it's important to make sure I'm around for emergencies and for your retirement. But the way you act, I don't think you'll *ever* be able to enjoy me, no matter how much of me you have. I like to make people happy—but right now, I feel like I'm in prison!

ME: I see that, but when my dad lost all that money in the stock market and got so depressed, I swore I'd never let that happen to me. I just can't relax until I've saved all the money I can—and even then I don't know if it'll be enough.

MONEY: Boy, are you a tough case! Lighten up and smell the roses, will you?

Commentary

MOTHER: Keep it up, son! If you don't keep saving, you could lose everything as your dad did. And you know how being poor destroyed his life and his confidence. The only way you can be safe is to keep sacrificing present comforts for future security.

FATHER: If I hadn't lost all that money, we'd have been happy. Hold onto every penny, my boy—and don't let any chump talk you into squandering it!

WIFE: You're cramping my style so much that, like Money, I can't breathe! I hate living in such an atmosphere of worry and miserliness. Honey, the crash of '29 was over half a century ago. Let's start enjoying life today, before it's too late!

HIGHER POWER: My child, you are out of balance in the way you think about spending and saving. I'm pleased that you've taken the gifts I gave you and made them productive through your hard work, but they are meant to nourish you and your family today as well as tomorrow. If you insist on hoarding the money you earn and making your family live cheerlessly, you may end up rich in assets—but poor in spirit, and in the family and friends who are the real treasures of a happy life.

By listening to our own inner dialogues, we help ourselves transform negative beliefs and attitudes into more positive and productive ones. The voice of our Higher Power, and sometimes the voice of Money itself, can show us the way toward more balance and money harmony. My clients almost always find their money dialogues to be extremely powerful tools for self-awareness and growth. I recommend you write a new conversation every week to monitor changes in your relationship with Money.

At first, you may feel too vulnerable to share these dialogues with your partner. If so, create them solely for your own enlightenment and see if you're comfortable sharing some of the lessons you learn from them.

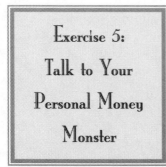

Exercise 5:

Talk to Your

Personal Money

Monster

Another creative way to come to grips with a money compulsion is to imagine that it's a monster, or maybe a creature from outer space, that has been controlling your behavior. In this exercise, I suggest that each partner prepare a dialogue imagining a confrontation with his or her own "money monster." Here's one spender's dialogue.

MONEY MONSTER: I'm so glad you're in my power. I really have fun messing with your head. Just when things seem calm, I can jerk your chain and make you want to go out and shop. What a blast!

ME: I really loathe the power you have over me.

MONEY MONSTER: It's such a gas to watch you flail around under my spell. Like the time you went into that department store to buy jeans for your kid—remember?—and walked out with your head spinning, your pulse racing, and $200 worth of clothes for yourself under your arm. Wow, was that fun!

ME: Yes—and I hated myself when I got home. This is infuriating! Why are you doing this to me?

MONEY MONSTER: Oh, I dunno. It keeps me busy. I guess I feel bored, empty . . . kinda starved.

ME: Starved for what?

MONEY MONSTER: Maybe to do something meaningful. Or to live more meaningfully—to give more to others and be more receptive to them. You know, you don't slow down and enjoy life;

you're always rushing around, crossing things off your "to do"
list. You ought to take more time to just listen to yourself.

ME: Okay, I'll try. Next time you try to pull my strings in a mall,
I'll just sit down, breathe deeply, and spend a little time with
myself.

MONEY MONSTER: Hmm. Okay, I guess that sounds good to me.

In this case, I didn't suggest a commentary because my client
had already begun the healing process in her dialogue. But if your
own dialogue doesn't seem to be leading anywhere, take this exercise another step by imagining how your mother, your father, and
your Higher Power (or inner voice of wisdom) might comment on
what you and your Money Monster have said to each other.

This exercise can really stretch your
imagination. I want you to imagine
yourself feeding your money monster
with more and more of what it desires.
Write a description or draw a picture of
your monster. (One client even clipped
photos from a magazine and glued
them into a collage depicting her personal money monster.)

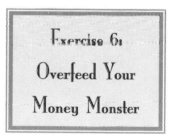

Exercise 6:

Overfeed Your

Money Monster

* What does your money monster look like? (Is it a "he," a "she,"
or an "it"?)

* What kind of sound(s) does it make?

* What would it feel like if you touched it?

- What does it feed on?

- What (if anything) would make it satisfied?

To figure out what this monster feeds on, ask yourself what sustains your money behavior. If you're a spender, your monster might feed on your feeling that you deserve to have everything you want. If you're a hoarder, you might see the monster feeding on your worries about the future: a medical emergency that could force you to quit your job, a stock market crash that might wipe out your investments, a layoff at work, the bank repossessing the house, the IRS seizing your assets.

Once you've figured out what your money monster feeds on, imagine giving it what it wants—but in some way that wouldn't harm you. For example, if your monster feeds on your need to have the beautiful clothes and other things you never had in childhood, envision feeding it haute couture clothes you'd never wear and expensive objects that aren't to your taste.

In your mind's eye, keep feeding the monster . . . and feeding . . . and feeding . . . and feeding some more, even after it's become sated. What happens to your all-powerful money monster when it's overfed?

This visualization exercise can be a lot of fun, and revealing as well. I think you'll enjoy watching your monster lose its power.

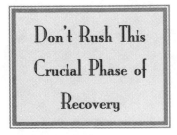

Don't Rush This Crucial Phase of Recovery

Sometimes as you're working on your money history, a money dialogue, or a money monster conversation, a light bulb will go off in your head: *Aha! So* **that's** *why I feel this way!* Or as you look through your spending journal, a pattern will pop out at you: *So* **that's** *what sets off my urge to spend!* Even reviewing your financial situation can produce moments of revelation: *Good grief, so* **that's** *where so much of our money's going!*

These magic moments are what therapists hope for, because an understanding of your habits and your motivations is crucial to the recovery process. But if you haven't had a breakthrough, don't be discouraged, even though you may be feeling impatient and frustrated by your slow progress in self-discovery. Instead, stick with these exercises a while longer. Keep trying to be more open and honest with yourself. In your moneytalks, encourage your partner to ask sympathetic questions that may help you view things from a different angle.

Sooner or later, in almost every case, the lightbulb will click on. By its light, you'll be able to see your overspending compulsion more clearly—and be able to start taking effective steps to overcome it.

10.

Fighting Off Temptation

If the awareness exercises in chapter 9 have exposed some of the circumstances or emotions that trigger your spending urge, you've taken a tremendously important step toward recovery. For example, if you now realize that you were scarred by emotional deprivation or financial catastrophe in childhood and that these wounds hurt especially when you're feeling overworked, unappreciated, or angry at your partner, you're much closer to finding ways to short-circuit your spending compulsion before it can set off another binge.

That's what this chapter is all about. I've divided it into two parts: short-term tactics that work immediately at what we might call the POT (point of temptation); and long-term strategies that will quite literally change your life. But first, I want to call your attention to a powerful temptation-fighting strategy that can work for you on the spot *and* over the long haul.

Goals can be primarily financial or primarily personal. It may be a good idea for you to choose one of each kind, so that you're working on both of them at the same time.

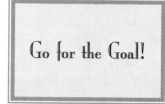

A financial goalplan consists of figuring out something you'd rather "buy" with your money than the impulse purchases that tempt you on your shopping expeditions. For example, let's say you (and your partner, if appropriate) decide that your financial goal will be to save $5,000 over the next two years for the down payment on a house.

Because you've reviewed your financial status report in a recent moneytalk, you already know the only way you can save this much money in this time is to cut back on your spending. Having calculated how much you'll need to put aside each month, you or your partner will make arrangements to have this amount automatically deposited into savings from a paycheck or checking account.

Can you reduce your spending enough to cover this savings contribution? You bet you can, if the goal of buying a home is meaningful and important enough to you.

To make it work, you'll need just two things: a small notebook like the one you used for your spending journal and a picture of your dream house (or a likeness that's as close to it as you can find). Carry these two items with you everywhere—everywhere cash, checks, or credit cards are accepted, anyway. Whenever you're sorely tempted to spend, open up your notebook and write down the item you're lusting after and how much it costs ("Camel hair blazer, $95").

Then take out your home picture and begin imagining yourself walking up the front steps and through your own front door. Imagine as vividly as you can the spacious kitchen, the cozy den, the

built-in bookshelves . . . all the details you've longed for in your
dream house. Say firmly to yourself, "I'm going to buy a piece of
my house today."

Then close your notebook and walk away.

By inspiring you to *want* to cut your discretionary spending,
having a goal subtly encourages the disciplines of deferred gratification and voluntary saving.

For this strategy to truly benefit you financially and psychologi-
cally, there are a couple of rules to follow. First, no cheating by
claiming "credit" for purchases you're not really tempted to make.
Second, no adding up of dollar amounts (for several months, at
least) to see if you've reached your monthly savings "quota." This
could prompt an irresistible impulse to start spending again—kind
of like diving into a triple hot-fudge sundae once you realize you've
reached your weight-loss goal.

A personal goalplan is based on a decision to broaden the horizons of your life. I believe it's important to work on a personal goal
in tandem with a financial one for the goal-setting process to be
truly life-changing.

Why? Because your financial plan—effective as it may be in
reducing your consumption—is like a diet you begin so you'll look
good in a swimsuit by July. Unless you're able to change your habits fundamentally and positively in the interim, once you reach
your goal you're likely to ease right back into your original pump-
kin shape by Halloween.

Your personal goal should serve as a catalyst of positive, long-
term change: an achievement that will challenge you, add creative
fulfillment or meaning to your life, and provide deeper, more grati-
fying nourishment than a spending binge's adrenaline surge.

Here are some examples of a personal goal you might commit
to, working out a step-by-step program in a realistic time frame:

* If you're tired of being a couch potato, you might set a goal (with your doctor's blessing) of getting in shape to handle a five-kilometer road race, a country-roads tour with your local bike club, or a hike up some challenging but manageable mountain.

* If you're computer shy, your goal might be to become proficient enough to manage your money, write letters, and play a game on your family PC.

* If you've always wanted to follow in the footsteps of Van Gogh, you might combine a personal goal with a financial one by deciding to brush up on your French, take a painting class at your local museum or art school, and save enough for a trip to Provence.

As with your financial goal, carry some inspiring reminder of your personal goal (a postcard of Van Gogh's "Starry Night," say), which you can use to renew your resolve when tempted by an impulse to shop or spend.

As you reach your goals, start right away on a plan for some new achievement. (Of course, the success of a personal goal may mean you're less tempted to shop. Congratulations! Now your financial goal can become a straightforward savings effort.)

James Bond's heart is racing, his hands are sweating, and his face is pale as he stares down at the digital clock on the A-bomb to which Goldfinger has handcuffed him—a bomb *(tick tick tick)* that is about to blow up Fort Knox, not to mention his own suave self, unless he can figure out how to stop the countdown.

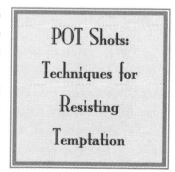

POT Shots:

Techniques for

Resisting

Temptation

Have you ever felt like this at a store counter . . . or at your kitchen table with a catalog in one hand and the phone in the other? The temptation to buy is so powerful it can make you feel completely helpless, caught up in a seemingly unstoppable chain reaction. If you could only slow it down, you might stand a chance—but chances are, you may not feel you can even do that. Is there no way to disarm this ticking bomb before it's too late?

The answer is emphatically *yes*. In this section, I've outlined four ways you can teach yourself to react in a different, more positive way when you're in a POT situation.

Which of these four techniques will work best for you? There's really no way to know ahead of time. In describing them, I've given examples to help you envision what they might be able to do for you. Caution: It could be a mistake to try just the ones that sound easy or comfortable to do. My clinical experience shows that often the greatest progress results from doing what you find most difficult or most unhabitual. (One client jokingly refers to this as "Mellan's Law of Being Where You Ain't Now.")

TAKING OVER THE "RADIO STATION"

I discovered this unusual compulsion-blocking technique when I asked a spender client to describe the sound she heard when she was embarking on a binge or was in the middle of one. She said at once, "I hear a voice saying over and over, 'Spinning around, spinning around, spinning around . . .' "

As an experiment, I asked her to try something the next time she began to sense a desire to spend. She was to say to herself the message her "binge broadcaster" would soon be beaming to her: "Spinning around, spinning around, spinning around . . ."

She did it—and the urge to shop that had been building up inside her fizzled completely.

Another spender told me she often felt compelled to go on binges after having lunch with her mother, or even after a phone conversation with her. Her mother's constant faultfinding and carping, the daughter said, gave her the screaming meemies. "That's just what it makes me feel like, too," she added, and imitated the binge-triggering sound she heard in her head after contact with her mother, a shrill, eerie sound like a soprano chain saw: "Mimimimimimi . . . !

I suggested she try my "taking over the radio station" technique. The next time she lunched with her mother, as the acidulous criticism began to build up insecurity, tension, and the urge to shop for comfort inside her, she quietly excused herself from the table, went to the ladies' room, and in a cubicle by herself said out loud, "Mimimimimimi . . . !"

It worked. The tension evaporated as if by magic, and she was able to finish lunch without her usual rush to the nearest store afterward. By co-opting the sound of her own compulsion, she'd taken over the radio station and put the binge broadcaster off the air.

See if you can identify the spending message your internal broadcaster has been sending you. If so, you may be able to use it yourself to take control of the airwaves.

JAMMING THE TRIGGER

I like this term of Susan Forward's, which so vividly describes the temptation-avoiding tactics you need to practice.[1] To jam the trigger successfully and prevent the urge to spend from taking you over, it's important to work out nondestructive alternatives that will give you the rewards or consolation you crave.

As we've discussed, having a meaningful personal and/or financial goal can help you jam the "spend" message. As you brainstorm other ideas by yourself or with your partner, think about the activities in your life that give you real, inner pleasure (or would if you made more time for them). When the temptation to shop or spend strikes, consider such trigger-jamming options as these:

- Calling a friend you really enjoy talking to.
- Reading a book strictly for fun.
- Writing down your thoughts and feelings.
- Taking a long walk in the fresh air (practice deep breathing and mindful awareness of what it feels like to be inside your body).
- Going to a museum you've meant to visit for a long time.
- Going to a movie or renting a favorite old film on video.
- Exercising in a way you enjoy.
- Calling your partner and proposing a date for lunch or dinner.
- Taking a kid to the zoo.
- Grubbing around in your garden.
- Writing a long letter to your former college roommate, or to someone else you love but haven't been in touch with lately.

These following activities also work particularly well for me:

- Singing in the car and/or listening to music I love.
- Slowing the process of impulsive shopping by writing things down: my feelings about why I need to buy whatever I feel like rushing out

and buying, alternative ways to meet this need, how much will it cost, do I really have the money now, and how would I feel if I didn't buy it (all ways to try to factor this emotional purchase into my logical moneylife).

* Closing my eyes and doing some relaxation breathing exercises that help me slow down and settle into myself.

* Going to my ballroom dancing lessons, which often leave me feeling so energized and happy that the urge to shop is minimized, if not eliminated completely.

* Volunteering to cuddle "boarder babies" at a local facility, a wonderfully calming experience.

* Painting watercolors of flowers from real life, a deeply fulfilling activity inspired by reading *The Artist's Way: A Spiritual Path to Higher Creativity*, by Julia Cameron with Mark Bryan. By giving me a sense of self-nurturing that no amount of shopping can equal, this creative pursuit has cut back powerfully on my urge to splurge.

All of these can be wonderful substitutes for compulsive spending.

BOOKENDING

This is the term Debtors Anonymous uses for their temptation-fighting technique. It's not a typical POT tactic, because you need to initiate it when you first feel the desire to shop begin to creep into your consciousness. Instead of jumping in the car to head for the mall, call a friend who's also in the DA program. Make a commitment to this "buddy" (who as far as we're concerned could be your partner) that you'll resist the urge to go shopping.

Then, work on jamming the trigger by focusing on some alternative activity, or perhaps just sit quietly, listening to your favorite music, and recenter yourself. When you feel calm and in control, call your buddy back to report that you were successful in sticking to your decision not to shop. Enjoy the satisfaction of knowing you were able to strengthen yourself a little bit more this time.

STOP, LOOK, AND LISTEN

This is Gloria Arenson's phrase for the overall strategy we're putting in place here.[2] Through the six awareness exercises you did in chapter 9, you've learned to *stop* (as you did when writing down your expenditures in your spending diary), *look* (as you did in reviewing your money history, your financial status report, and your daily expenditures), and *listen* (as you did in "hearing" the dialogues between yourself, Money, and your money monster).

A special listening therapy Arenson suggests is called "changing the tape." For example, suppose you're thinking rather nervously about a party you'll be attending this weekend. From inside, you hear a voice urging you to go out and buy a new jacket for the occasion, so you can be sure to make a good impression. But as a spender, you've learned to recognize this old taped message. And so you consciously elect to change the tape, substituting new messages like these:

- I'll have a good time if I decide to, no matter what I wear.

- I'd rather have people like me for my intelligence, friendliness, and sense of humor than because I'm wearing a new jacket.

* I don't have to look perfect to be accepted.

* I already own jackets that look just fine.

The idea of "stop, look, and listen" works on several levels: a behavioral one, an emotional one, and an intellectual one, as well as an inner-power level that is the product of the other three. In other words, when push comes to shove and you're struggling with a hunger to fill yourself up with "things," *stop* your immediate impulse to head for the shopping center or to whip out your credit card (if the countdown has gone that far) . . . sit down, breathe deeply, and *look* at what this impulse is trying to tell you. Choose to *listen* to a different tape that gives you healthier, more positive ways to fulfill your needs.

It's easy to become intimidated by the foreverness of the future. With the world ateem with beckoning storefronts and alluring advertisements, chock-full of so many things you'd love to have for your own, will you ever be stalwart enough to pass them by without a second glance?

> Turning "I Won't" Power into "I Will" Power: Long-Term Tips for Spenders

By being committed enough to read this far, you've shown you're not afraid to face the fact that in most cases, real healing is a long-haul process. And it's important to realize that despite your growing awareness of the reasons for your spendaholic behavior and the new responses you're trying to learn, it will take time to overcome the anguish of deprivation attacks—those inner tantrums whose silent shriek is "I won't!"

The impact of these attacks will probably be strongest a few weeks after you've begun your program, once the first surge of enthusiasm has waned and at moments when you're at your lowest ebb—tired after a long, hard workday, frustrated by your partner's seeming neglect, or angry at the heavy demands of your family or other responsibilities.

At times like these, this inner protest can be powerful enough to turn steely resolution into limp spaghetti. You can almost hear the deprived child in you banging its fists on the floor, yelling, "It's not fair! I work hard! I make sacrifices all day long for my job, my partner, my kids—I deserve what you buy me! If you don't show you love me, who can I count on?" Or you may hear your money monster bellowing, "I'm hungry! I feel empty! Feed me!"

My goal in this section is to help you establish long-term recovery patterns that can supply the healthier nourishment needed to wean your "monster" from its addiction to spending. By integrating the tips, exercises, and activities in the next pages into your life, you'll find it easier to maintain your progress toward money harmony.

PRACTICE THE NONHABITUAL

To learn new actions along with the new attitudes you're developing, I suggest taking on a homework assignment each week. Your objective in working on these exercises should be to gradually integrate into your life the new behavior you practice each week.

You'll learn even more if you take the time to write down your feelings in your money notebook or journal—hopefully *before*, perhaps *during*, and definitely *after* these assignments. For example, was the new experience enjoyable? If so, what felt good about it? If not, what emotions did you feel, and why do you think you felt them? Did your feelings change after you tried the assignment more than once?

Here are some homework assignments you might undertake.[3]

- Put money in savings.

- Put money in an envelope or in a wallet compartment and don't spend it for at least a month.

- Pay off all or part of a debt that's been hanging over your head.

- Leave your credit cards at home for a week.

- Promise yourself that before making any unplanned purchase costing more than $10, you'll write down in your journal the pros and cons of buying it, and think about it for twenty-four hours.

- Before making any unplanned purchase of any size, physically walk away from the item, leave the store, and think about it for at least ten minutes.

- Comparison-shop price and quality in three locations before making any unplanned purchase over $10.

- Put an impulse item on layaway instead of buying it outright, so you have the latitude to change your mind and cancel your purchase after you've had a chance to think about it calmly.

- Take the time to give a pleasurable experience to a child, partner, or friend instead of buying an expensive gift. For example, pack a picnic, rent a canoe at a nearby state park, and go for an afternoon paddle on a pond or river. Or put together a personalized cassette tape made up of music the recipient especially loves or can relate to, linked by your own commentary. Emotionally meaningful gifts like these can become memories that are beyond price.

I urge you to expand your repertoire of new attitudes and actions by inventing assignments of your own that force you to "be where you ain't now." Like pumping iron, these homework exercises can build your strength and confidence—and help reeducate the inner voice that has been shrilly predicting misery and suffering if you don't get what you want.

SEEK ALTERNATIVE WAYS TO MEET YOUR DEEPER NEEDS

You may never be able to forget the early experiences that shaped your needs and behavior (such as growing up with a dictatorial dad who was an obsessive hoarder), but you do have the power to alter the way you respond to those needs.

Instead of feeding your money monster by spending money, find longer-term ways to enhance your self-esteem and give yourself pleasure. If you haven't already set a personal goal to help you with this need, here are a few suggestions.[4] (Thanks to my friend Vicki Robin for some of these ideas.)

- Enrich your knowledge by taking a course in something you've always wanted to know about (basic car maintenance, CPR, furniture antiquing, cabinetmaking).

- Choose a subject to study for the sheer challenge of it (Mandarin Chinese, writing haiku, playing the bagpipes).

- Expand your senses by learning to sing or play a musical instrument, sculpt or paint, or tune in to the natural world around you.

- Join a club or group to learn more about a special interest of yours (Civil War history, Dixieland jazz, local historic site preservation) and meet fellow fans. No such club in your area? Start one!

⁕ Share your knowledge and experience by helping others as a Big Brother, Big Sister, literacy tutor, or whatever form of volunteering feels best to you.

Don't forget to carry a reminder of this nourishing new behavior with you, to refresh you when you're tempted to slide back into your old mall-hopping habits. For example, you might glance now and then at your CPR certification card, a note with "I can read this!" written on it in Chinese, or a photo of your Little Sister or Little Brother.

MINIMIZE YOUR EXPOSURE TO SLIPPERY PLACES

You now should have a good idea what situations, states of mind, or physical locales predispose you to a spending binge. (Alcoholics Anonymous members call these "slippery places.") If you can't avoid these danger zones, try to neutralize whatever specific aspect of them shoves you into a skid.

Note that there may be more than one possible way to stay on your feet in a slippery place. Or you may choose to line up several alternatives behind each other, so that if Plan A doesn't work, you can fall back on Plan B, and so on. For example:

Trigger: exposure to a danger zone (the mall, where you've decided to look for a birthday gift for your niece). Possible solutions:

⁕ Prepare a list of three or four alternative gift ideas and the stores where these gifts might be found. Stick closely to this list as you move through the mall.

* Take a supportive friend with you to help you resist other impulse purchases.

* Before you leave for the mall, tell your partner or a buddy that you plan not to buy anything on impulse for yourself or others. Let this person know you'll contact him or her to confirm this when you return.

* Forestall temptation by avoiding the mall and shopping in one or two smaller stores instead.

Trigger: the frustrations of a dull, dead-end job. Possible solutions:

* Challenge your boss by requesting and justifying specific new responsibilities.

* Update your resumé and begin networking to seek more rewarding work elsewhere.

* Both of these.

Trigger: resentment of an overly controlling partner. Possible solutions:

* Volunteer to help your partner practice letting go. For example, take over paying the bills in alternate months. Alternate being driver and passenger. Take turns being "host" for an evening out, deciding where to go, where to sit, how much to tip when you pay the bill.

* Jointly explore a new area of interest where you're both neophytes.

* Develop your own field of expertise.

* "Take over the radio station" and refuse to let this behavior bug you.

Note that some triggers are physical and others are emotional. Whichever the source, both can be dangerous to an overspender.

KEEP UP YOUR JOURNAL TO
MONITOR YOUR CHANGES

As you work on resolving trigger situations and adopting new ways of meeting your deeper needs, keep using your money notebook to record your thoughts, ideas, and feelings in response to your changing attitudes and actions. This allows you to track progress (and old resistances as well), while reminding you in a very concrete way that recovery happens one day at a time.

Remember, no one else needs to see this record but you—so try to drop any defensiveness or denial you may have, and confide in it openly. When you're honest and regular in your entries, a journal can be both empowering and liberating. On days when you've succeeded in changing your behavior, you'll have the satisfaction of putting it down in black and white, and you can take a moment to give yourself credit for your courage and determination.

If your progress isn't so evident on another day, writing down exactly what happened can help you learn from it. Were there special circumstances that caused you to backslide? Were you in a particular emotional state? How can you recognize this sort of situation and deal with it better next time?

Then, after learning all you can from what you did that day, you can turn the page and start fresh tomorrow.

Keep writing in your journal as long as the process continues to benefit you. Some people have kept their notebooks going for months or years, as a disciplined way to stay in touch with themselves and track their progress toward money harmony.

REWARD NEW ACTIONS AND ATTITUDES

For every assignment done, consider rewarding yourself with something that doesn't cost much money, or perhaps costs nothing. These perks might include:

- Dates with your partner. Think of the fun things you used to do when you were getting to know each other (which were usually cheap if you didn't have much money then).

- Lunching with a friend at a place you can afford.

- Calls to friends or family far away.

- A long relaxing bath with your favorite music in the background and a book or magazine you've been looking forward to reading.

- Going to a movie, stage show, or concert.

- Visiting an art, science, or historical museum.

- A walk in the woods.

- Taking a slow, conscious shopping trip with a friend, during which you make a preplanned purchase for yourself with a spending limit in mind.

This last suggestion may seem to be putting you right in the path of temptation, but I believe that slow, deliberate spending can be a healing and strengthening experience. Though some recovering spenders can handle a solo trip to a store, the physical presence of a loving friend you trust can be especially valuable during the beginning of the recovery process. Accompanied by someone who understands and supports your need to stop overspending, you'll find it easier to visit a store without going into a trance and losing control of your rational decision-making powers.

∾

Two Organizations That Can Help You Help Yourself

Debtors Anonymous is a network of local self-help groups patterned on Alcoholics Anonymous. No dues or fees are charged; instead, members pass the hat at meetings to cover the group's expenses. Anyone with a debt problem is welcome to attend anytime.

DA credits the success of its program to two elements: the support and encouragement of others who have struggled with compulsive indebtedness, and a strong belief in a Higher Power who can "restore us to sanity." Its meetings offer debtors a safe place in which they can gain a sense of hope, identify with others who have made the journey, and meet people who can help. As the name promises, you're anonymous—known only by your first name—an aspect of DA that relieves some spenders who feel ashamed or embarrassed by their chaotic financial life.

After attending a certain number of DA meetings to familiarize yourself with the ground rules, you'll start working in what DA calls a "pressure group"—a task force made up of you and two other experienced, currently abstinent DA members that will focus on developing an action plan to deal with your creditors, a spending plan to stop you from taking on new debt, and a repayment plan to retire your existing debt gradually.

Debtors Anonymous says, "Our experience has shown that the DA program will always work for any person who has a desire to stop using debt."5 To find the nearest DA chapter in your area, call (212) 642-8220, or write to:

Debtors Anonymous
P.O. Box 400, Grand Central Station
New York, NY 10163-0400.

Consumer Credit Counseling Service (CCCS) are a group of companies around the country affiliated with the National Foundation for Consumer Credit. In 1993, more than one million consumers called CCCS offices for help, and over two-thirds of them signed up for free counseling.

In these counseling sessions, CCCS caseworkers encourage sensible money habits for people who just need a little guidance to get back on their feet. In a CCCS booklet that shows you how to put together a realistic spending plan, these sensible habits are codified into "Twelve Rules for Successful Money Management," which include such common-sense commandments as these:

* A spending plan does not prevent you from getting what you want; it *helps* you get what you want.

* Decide what your family's most important goals are. Your money should be spent for those things that mean most to your family's welfare and happiness, and not wasted on things that mean least to you and your family.

* Bring all the family into the plan. If every family member understands the family goals, they will work harder for them and your plan will stand a better chance of success. It is important that any major purchase first be discussed and mutually agreed upon.

* Pay yourself first by trying to save 10 percent of your income. If you can't manage 10 percent right away, try to save a smaller amount, but do so regularly.

If your debt problem is so overwhelming that a self-help program won't work, you can ask CCCS to develop a Debt Management Plan for you. DMPs are serious, very strict repayment plans that should be used only as a last resort before bankruptcy. (In fact, CCCS notes that two of every three clients who fail to live by their DMP eventually do file for bankruptcy.)

In the DMP program—used by more than 300,000 consumers in 1993—CCCS does a complete analysis of your income and debts and works out an individualized payment plan. They'll negotiate with your creditors to forgo interest and penalties, extend repayment periods, and sometimes accept lesser amounts, as long as you stick with your DMP—a deal creditors usually accept, knowing that the most likely alternative is getting nothing if you go bankrupt. This arrangement tends to reduce your net monthly outlay for debt repayment.

Every month until you're out of the woods, you send a check for the agreed-on amount to CCCS, and they'll pay your bills according to your DMP agreement. It's not easy—you must learn to get by with only a fraction of the disposable income you freely spent before. But millions of spenders have used this program to get free of debt, avoiding the sense of defeat and financial stigma of declaring bankruptcy, and gaining the self-confidence and satisfaction of having restored themselves to solvency.[6]

For the location of the CCCS office nearest you, call 1-800-388-2227.

∾

> ### The Secret of Long-Term Success: Do Your Best *Today*

As you work through the process of transforming yourself into a calmer, more rational spender, remember two things. First, open up to people who care about you and your struggle and may be happy to help you—like the shopping buddy I just mentioned.

Second, take one day at a time. The thought of changing your familiar patterns of behavior "forever" can be a scary one. Just resolve to do things differently *for today*. If you succeed, great! The vow you make the next morning—to resist your overspending urges *for today*—may be a little easier to keep. And if you have a setback, it's not the end of the world. When you wake up the next morning, you can once again resolve to change your behavior *for today*.

Many recovery programs stress the familiar phrase: "Today is the first day of the rest of your life." It's really true—and by trying to make every "today" a day that strengthens and nourishes you, you'll be on your way to long-term recovery.

PART FIVE

∾

The Long and Winding
Road

11.

Five Who Overcame

In the five case histories that follow, you'll read how ideas and exercises like the ones in this book have helped some of my therapy clients overcome overspending. (To protect their privacy and the confidentiality of our work together, I've changed their names and some identifying details.)

As you'll see, these individuals and couples worked hard to uncover the roots of their spending problems, and were willing and persistent in learning how to rebalance their moneylives. Perhaps you'll find situations here that are not unlike yours . . . and by learning from these spenders' examples, be inspired to add your success to theirs.

Sheila was born to a hardscrabble farm family, the third of seven children. When she was in second grade her dad lost the farm, and they all moved to a cramped little house in town so he could take a factory job.

Win/Win Spending Control: The Story of Sheila and Ken

Her memories of that time were of desperate stress: her father trying to drink away his sense of failure, her mother trying to make the home a haven where he could find contentment, both of them constantly fighting about money. Angry and exhausted, they seldom paid much attention to her. Sheila tried to stay out of her parents' way, took care of the younger kids, and went to school in hand-me-downs. Seeing her classmates in new clothes and knowing they had easier lives, she vowed to herself that one day she would escape her deprived surroundings and have the money to buy everything she wanted.

With hard work and the help of student loans, Sheila managed to go to college and graduate with a degree in education. Although she didn't earn much money as a teacher, she gloried in spending it on gorgeous clothes that made her feel like one of the kids she'd envied in her childhood.

After these shopping binges, she would float along for a while on a gratification high. Life seemed fine until she married Ken, when her unwillingness to budget and her compulsive overspending caught up with her at last. When she finally had the courage to add up the debts that had mounted over the years, they totaled nearly $65,000. Ashamed of her irresponsible behavior and afraid for the stability of her marriage, Sheila was deeply depressed when she and Ken sought therapy.

Fortunately, Ken was exactly the sort of loving, understanding partner she needed. They agreed that solving the problem was their shared responsibility, since they had both contributed to it—Sheila by overspending, and Ken by trustingly going along with her behavior and letting her control their money.

We decided that I would see Sheila individually and that she would also join a Debtors Anonymous group and attend its weekly meetings. Whenever we felt it would be helpful, Ken would join us in therapy sessions to support Sheila as she worked to turn around her overspending.

One of the first steps Sheila took was to begin writing down all her expenditures. This helped her get in touch with the real details of her moneylife by discovering exactly where her money was going.

Next, I asked her to note down all her childhood memories about money and to write a money dialogue, which we discussed at our next session. These exercises helped her recognize her still-intense resentment of her father's alcoholism and resulting coldness. It also deepened her awareness of the revenge motive that prompted her to overspend to get back at him and everyone else who had tried to deprive her. As she came to understand how spending had become a substitute for the love and happiness of which she'd felt cheated, Sheila saw that this behavior had actually been eroding her self-esteem over the years, testing the love of those who did care for her, and putting at risk her chance of real happiness.

With these insights, Sheila at last had the self-awareness she needed to turn her life around. Her solid relationship with Ken, who was open, nonjudgmental, and willing to cooperate in her healing progress, gave her the support she needed to move ahead quickly on a plan to reduce her debt.

Later, she told me a story that illustrated the win/win spirit with which this couple approached managing their problem. As she and Ken were walking into a crafts fair one day, he told her, "Now remember, honey, we can't spend any money here." Sheila was immediately gripped by her old feelings of rebellion against forced deprivation; she urgently wanted to buy something, anything, just to assert her independence.

However, new self-awareness from her therapy exercises made her pause a moment and say calmly to Ken, "When you say it that way, I feel as though I'm in a straitjacket. It would help me if you'd say instead, 'Honey, let's try to spend only a small amount of money here; why don't we set a limit together?' Then I could feel fine maybe buying something small, or even buying nothing at all." Ken agreed that this made sense. They set a limit of $10, ended up buying something for $8, and both felt satisfied.

Since starting therapy, Sheila has managed to reduce her debt by 75 percent. Family gifts have helped, but she's proudest of the contribution made by her persistence in developing and sticking to a spending plan. She continues to attend DA meetings, and is learning to nurture herself in other, more fulfilling ways.

Clearly, one of Sheila's advantages was having the help of a supportive, loving partner. It's important that caring partners like Ken don't feel they must become a jailer or permanent naysayer. If this happens, the spender begins to see the partner as the critical "bad parent," and sooner or later feels driven to rebel. A gentle reminder that both of you agreed to set spending limits can be much more effective during the fragile early-recovery stage.

We've talked in earlier chapters about the spender's right to be responsible for his or her own choices, and the crippling effect of being sheltered from reality by an overcontrolling partner. In the next case I'll share with you, this young client had been "helped" by his father to the point where he felt totally incapable of doing anything with money—except spending it quickly.

Eclipse of the Son: The Story of Jonathan and His Father

Life for young Jonathan was dominated by his father, a wealthy entrepreneur whose gifts of money were often generous but wildly unpredictable due to the nature of his business. Lack of communication between Jonathan and his father contributed to Jon's feeling of being dwarfed by his father's power and success, while his sporadic financial support left Jon feeling confused and frustrated.

Unable to connect these seemingly random handouts to paternal love or approval of his achievements, Jonathan never developed the self-confidence to make wise decisions about money. He lived from windfall to windfall and floated from job to job. When his father gave him money, he would typically use it to go on a wild spending spree, take an expensive vacation, or buy extravagant gifts for his live-in girlfriend, Penny.

After years of these wild swings from loneliness and anxiety to brief periods of euphoria, Jon felt utterly incompetent to manage his financial life. When he started therapy, his debt from overspending was huge, his self-esteem was at an all-time low, and he was panicked about his ability to handle a new job opportunity that had just presented itself.

Jonathan and I began our sessions by preparing a family money history. He also wrote a money dialogue, which helped him see how he needed to change in order to come closer to money harmony. Through these awareness exercises, he realized that part of the reason he'd never tried to start a business of his own was fear of failing to measure up to the expectations of his father (who, in Jon's mind, had become an all-powerful and capricious authority).

Jon also recognized that if he continued this hand-to-mouth existence, he'd never start living his own life or accept responsibility for his own money choices. Unfortunately, his ability to change was cramped by the limiting patterns that had been rooted in him since childhood. Because he was spiritually oriented and very expressive, I suggested that he work with me through "Essence Repatterning."™ This powerful, intensive mental rewiring process, which was developed and taught to me by Pat McCallum,[1] helps people who are ready to change their destructive, self-sabotaging patterns turn the corner faster to begin healthier, more positive behavior.

A major breakthrough came when Jon invited his father to attend some of his therapy sessions. Much like Oz the Great and Terrible, Jonathan's father then stepped from behind the figurative curtain of noncommunication that had screened him from his son, revealing himself as a caring dad who hadn't realized the destructive impact of his preoccupation with work and the confusing messages his irregular support sent to Jon.

With open communication established with his father, Jonathan began to feel much more confident about taking the new job and learning to manage his money. He now uses personal-finance software to track his income and expenses, which makes him more conscious of his spending patterns. Therapy has also helped him become more open and honest with Penny, so she can better understand what's going on in his moneylife. In regular money meetings, they track their progress against a shared spending plan.

By opening up communication with his father and his partner and confronting his own sources of shame and fear, Jon has been able to curb his overspending dramatically. He recently took the major step of starting his own company. Though his father has willingly provided help and support, Jonathan is developing the inner strength and self-confidence to do his own thinking and planning before consulting his dad—a process that allows him to benefit from his father's competence without undermining his own. Now beginning to stand on his own feet financially, he feels better and better about himself every day.

Sheila's and Jonathan's stories show clearly how people may tie their self-image to the amount of money they control. Similarly, the sudden loss of money can translate into feelings that you yourself have lost value and will lose the respect of others (since you assume everyone feels as you do about money equaling esteem).

In circumstances like these, overspending can become a mask you hold up to reassure yourself and the rest of the world that everything's just fine. To heal, you must learn to do without the illusory shelter of that mask—which means distinguishing your real self from the myth that your status symbols represent who you are.

As Miranda's story demonstrates, this is a transformation that only you can bring about. If you sit around hoping somebody else will change reality for you, you may wait forever.

Miranda's family was relatively wealthy when she was growing up, thanks to her father's real estate investments. Then disaster struck—the bottom dropped out of the real estate market. As the value of his holdings plummeted, her dad began to drink more. Eventually, he lost his job, and they were forced to move from their

> Someday My Prince Will Come: The Story of Miranda and Joe

luxurious home to a small house in a middle-class neighborhood. For endless years, her father spiraled downward in a black depression that left Miranda, her brothers, and her mother feeling panicky and powerless.

At last, Miranda escaped by marrying Joe, a gentle, caring man who was then a middle manager in a struggling small business. Life seemed at last to be on an even keel, until Joe came home one day and told her he'd been laid off—and Miranda felt her childhood nightmare had once again become reality.

Joe had a hard time finding another full-time job. Though they weren't destitute, thanks to some consulting income he earned, along with investments and small family gifts, Miranda was overwhelmed with anxiety and depression because he wasn't bringing home a steady paycheck.

In a situation like this, most people would be understandably concerned about having to live for a long time without regular income. To Miranda, it was much worse. This financial hardship made her lose respect for her husband, although Joe's job loss was part of cutbacks due to the economy and not because of anything he'd done. Miranda's self-esteem shrank, too; deep inside, she felt devalued by her drop in financial status. Other people would respect her less, she believed, if they knew she and Joe had fallen on hard times.

And so she pretended to the outside world that everything was fine. She continued to spend money on luxurious home furnishings and on elegant and expensive clothing for herself and her three children, keeping her husband's financial trauma a closely guarded secret.

When Miranda and Joe consulted me, it was because her anger at Joe's joblessness was damaging their relationship, while her spending was overstressing their precarious financial situation. As we discussed their feelings and attitudes, Joe volunteered that he now found regular, structured work dull and boring; he much preferred the excitement and challenge of consulting, if he could just find a way to make a lot of money at it. This attitude only increased Miranda's anxiety and her compulsion to overspend, so no one would suspect Joe wasn't an excellent provider for his family.

Interestingly, Miranda herself was a talented professional illustrator. She wanted to begin illustrating children's books, but was paralyzed by the old childhood feelings of powerlessness and self-doubt that Joe's job loss had stirred up. These feelings made her focus on her husband's failure to provide a steady income, instead of letting her think about how she could use her creativity to achieve her professional ambitions and increase the income she herself earned. She avoided grappling with this opportunity by giving away her time and energy to everyone but herself, then wondered why she felt angry and resentful toward Joe and the kids at the end of the day.

Therapy helped unhook Miranda from her conviction that a good husband must by definition be the family's chief provider. By beginning to separate money from self-esteem, she felt more comfortable allowing her friends back into her life and not hiding the truth behind a façade of lavish spending. She was willing to postpone home renovation until she and Joe were really earning enough to pay for it—and gained the self-confidence to invite people over without worrying that her home wasn't perfect.

One of the most powerful moments in therapy for Miranda was when she visualized her money monster and began feeding it what it wanted, in larger and larger quantities. Miranda immediately conjured up a large green dinosaur devouring heaps of clothing and furniture. As the dinosaur kept eating, it grew more and more bloated and sluggish and finally rolled over on its side, clutching its belly. Now pitiful and comic, it lost its power to scare and dominate her.

After this assignment, her spending compulsion began to ease its grip. Another part of therapy that worked well for Miranda was discussing her unresolved childhood fears and anxieties in individual sessions with me. When Joe joined us in couples sessions, she was able to learn how to communicate with him positively and empathetically, instead of attacking him in a way that sapped his job-hunting enthusiasm even further. She also learned to express her deeper feelings more openly, and to tolerate her vulnerability without being panicked by it.

As a result of this hard work, Miranda was finally able to do something that was particularly hard for her: claiming and using her own creative talents to produce more income, instead of waiting for Joe to "save" her with a steady paycheck that would again make life seem safe and financially secure.

As Miranda's self-esteem grew, her spending declined—another sign that even though her story had taken a decidedly non-fairytale twist, she and Joe now had every chance of living happily ever after.

Miranda's story emphasizes once again that the money messages we tune in to as children stay with us for a lifetime. Even though they may be inaccurate, exaggerated, or wrong for us as adults, they tend to keep playing over and over like a broken record. As the next case shows, it's seldom easy to shut off these messages—but sometimes it's crucial if we're to find the money harmony we seek.

The Book Binger: The Story of Terry and Roger

Terry was the first one in her family to go to college. Over and over, her blue-collar father had impressed on her not to get her head in the clouds with dreams of some fancy career; the only way to be sure of having job security and a steady income, he said, was to work for the government.

A shy, studious book-lover, Terry didn't have the practical experience to contradict him. Not long after graduation, she ended up in Washington, D.C., working at a government job that paid moderately well but that she grew to hate over the years. The best thing about it, she felt now, was that it had enabled her to meet her husband, Roger, who was an auditor in another government agency.

Roger, however, was able to escape from his own dull job into two leisure-time passions: oil painting and art history. Terry envied his ability to immerse himself in the creative challenges of these hobbies for hours on end—a preoccupation that also left her feeling a little lonely and neglected. Without any creative outlet of her own, she began to resent the frustrations of her job more and more. However, her father's admonitions still rang in her ears; she felt she couldn't risk looking for another position outside of government, especially at her "advanced" age. (She was in her forties.)

Instead, Terry found herself spending more time in bookstores, buying all the books that might help her enrich her life—bags of books, armloads of books, stacks of books, more books than she could possibly read, containing all the knowledge she didn't have time to master because of her exhausting, boring job.

As the books piled up at home and the bills came in, Terry started having to juggle payments to cope with all her debts. This made her even more angry and resentful: her despised job didn't even pay enough to let her offset its boredom with the learning she craved! In a form of "revenge spending" against this hated authority figure (the job her father had essentially forbidden her to quit), she began buying even more books, along with the fine clothes and other amenities she felt she'd earned with her many years of obedience to her job.

When Terry started therapy, the first thing we did was explore the money messages she'd received in childhood, such as her father's insistence on safe, secure government employment. I suggested that Terry start keeping track of everything she spent money on. She also began opening up to her husband about her bill juggling and her book-buying binges, which had been screened from him by their separate financial arrangements. Roger willingly agreed to help her return books and manage her finances more responsibly, so she could save for the things she really wanted.

To satisfy her need for creative fulfillment, Terry learned to identify and participate in low- or no-cost creative activities she enjoyed, such as singing and needlework. Another therapy exercise we embarked on was generating a list of things she could do when the urge to go buy a particular book struck her, including calling friends, taking a walk, and writing down the reasons why she just had to have that book.

Terry's recovery wasn't effortless. For a while, she seesawed back and forth between book binges and more restrained behavior. Instead of attending Debtors Anonymous meetings and therapy sessions as often as recommended, she used the time and money to buy books. And it was almost impossible for her to consider looking for a job that would make her feel happier and more productive.

Finally, Terry realized the seriousness of her "bookaholism," and committed to weekly therapy sessions and Debtors Anonymous meetings. She began to return more books. At times, she asked Roger to help her by taking back the books for her, so she wouldn't be tempted to buy more while in the bookstore. She also completed a course in career change as the first step in moving toward more job fulfillment.

Initially, it was quite hard for Terry to get in touch with the feelings that took over before and after a book-buying binge. When I asked her to write down the emotions she felt, I found she was usually unable to stop herself for long enough before a binge to write anything down. Afterward, she tended to scourge herself over and over with expressions of shame, guilt, and self-hate.

Through our therapy sessions, Terry was able to delve deeper into the feelings, thoughts, and emotions that she felt only a shopping binge could relieve or fulfill. This has helped her understand what lies beneath her compulsion to spend and lets me help her find the courage to confront these feelings instead of trying to escape from them into overspending.

Terry is still struggling to recover, but she has turned a major corner. For the most part she has stopped buying books and no longer juggles her money to cover her bills. Her creative activities have expanded, and her relationship with her husband continues to deepen. Last but certainly not least, Terry recently began actively looking for a more rewarding, more fulfilling job.

Both in their 40s, Hector and Christine knew that if they were to have the children they wanted, they ought not to wait. But after six years of marriage, Christine found herself hesitant to make this commitment, worried about her uncertain financial future with the spendthrift husband she loved.

The Power of Love: The Story of Hector and Christine

Hector was affectionate, charming, and impulsive. A technological wizard whose corporate job paid $70,000 a year, he didn't seem to care how much he made—or how much he owed. With lavish spending on the latest computer equipment and frequent gifts for himself and Christine, he was sinking them ever deeper in debt. Month after month he ended up juggling bills and overdrawing their bank accounts.

Christine could hardly have been a greater contrast. A talented potter, she regularly asked too little money for her work. Furthermore, she was reluctant to spend anything on herself. After her inexpensive Timex wore out, she went for months without replacing it. When Hector bought her an expensive replacement watch for her birthday, she felt totally overwhelmed and unworthy of such a beautiful and costly gift.

Hector and Christine had read *Money Harmony* and recognized themselves as a spender/avoider and a hoarder/worrier. This difference in their money styles was the only source of tension in their relationship, but it was serious enough to prompt them to seek therapy.

To understand their attitudes better, we looked at their family backgrounds—a step that proved very enlightening.

The son of immigrants from Puerto Rico, Hector had grown up with no role models to show him the value of frugality, saving, or setting limits. His father, who had worked his way into a well-paid position as a researcher, enjoyed spending money on extravagant whims to show the world he had achieved status and success. His mother, a schoolteacher, had felt so guilty about leaving her three children with a baby-sitter while she was at work that she tended to buy them everything their hearts desired. Thus it was almost inevitable that Hector, the baby of the family, would eventually develop into an overspender and an avoider.

Christine, too, was just one generation away from poverty. Her father had been the only one of ten children in his farm family to go to college. Though he had become an engineer with a decent income, he behaved as if he were still very poor. Christine's mother, who had stayed home to raise Christine and her five siblings, never got enough money from her husband to meet all the family's needs. She scrimped, saved, and worried; and Christine too became a scrimper, saver, and worrier.

As different as Christine and Hector were, the saving grace this couple possessed was an extraordinarily loving and solid relationship. So when I asked each of them to write a money dialogue and "practice the nonhabitual," they were ready to take action.

Hector agreed to write down all his debts and to begin keeping a list of everything he spent money on. Christine wrote down her money worries and bought some small items for herself, noting her feelings about this unfamiliar self-indulgence.

By the next session, both reported that their tension and worry about money had eased. As Hector reviewed his family history and recorded his expenditures, he began to realize the extent of his overspending problem. Immensely relieved by his new awareness, Christine lovingly supported his first small (but significant) steps toward more balanced behavior. When he toyed with the impulse to buy something fairly extravagant, she found ways to suggest less costly alternatives.

For example, when they ate dinner in a restaurant Hector's habit was to order an appetizer, an entree, wine, and dessert. When Christine now suggested they just order an entree and either wine or dessert, he willingly agreed. He learned to cut back on spending at lunch, too. Instead of going out with friends every day and expansively picking up the entire tab, he began to take his lunch to work four days out of five, openly admitting to colleagues that he was trying to save money by not eating out as often.

Since beginning to change his behavior, Hector has also put together a schedule for paying off his debts and is keeping to it faithfully. All this has made Christine feel so much more secure that they are now thinking seriously of having children. "I always knew Hector would be a great father," Christine says. "But I worried about whether he'd be responsible about money. Now I feel surer and surer every day that I can rely on him."

Now that they are well on the road to recovery, Hector and Christine have tapered off to monthly therapy sessions, where they set new tasks and goals for themselves as each of them continues to move toward the middle. By understanding the roots of their money behavior, learning to communicate more effectively with each other, practicing the nonhabitual, and keeping track of their expenditures and emotions, they are creating their own success story.

Sheila and Ken, Jonathan and his father, Miranda and Joe, Terry and Roger, Hector and Christine, and the others you've met in this book have all traveled the road you're on now. Following the signposts of self-awareness, enduring the rough spots with compassion and the long stretches with persistence, they've set out toward a destination that promises deeper fulfillment and a happier life.

Journey's End

In India, there is an old tradition that at a certain stage in life, after the children are grown and married, a man may give away his house, his possessions, and every rupee he owns, and take to the open road with nothing but the clothes on his back and a begging bowl to seek the alms of passersby. Alone with no resources of his own, the beggar commits himself to a new life of simplicity, accepting what may befall him—rain, cold, hunger—with a serenity of spirit that allows him to exist in harmony with all other things.

Much more than geography separates us from this remarkable awareness that "things" can prevent us from living in harmony with ourselves and with the world around us. Growing up amid great abundance, many of us learned that possessions were actually an essential part of our self-definition.

Before you began *Overcoming Overspending*, this might have been your attitude, too. I hope you're now beginning to see life differently, to recognize that much of our compulsive buying and spending is just an attempt to satisfy a voice within us crying, "I'm hungry! I'm empty! Feed me!"

Hoping to satisfy this hunger for fulfillment and happiness, we try to fill ourselves up with possessions and entertainment. But each fast-fleeting pleasure leaves us even hungrier, so we consume more and more: a bigger house, a faster boat, smarter clothes, more self-indulgent services, more exotic vacations.

During my twenty-plus years of experience in doing therapy work with clients, trying to heal myself, and observing friends, family, and passersby in my world, I've concluded that true happiness and fulfillment do not follow from an abundance of money or the things money can buy.

Yes, money is important—no one is saying you need to huddle penniless under a highway bridge to find Nirvana. But more important than money are the ways we succeed in making ourselves open to life: learning to accept and respect ourselves; fostering meaningful friendships; nurturing and strengthening an intimate relationship with a partner we love; sharing ourselves with the community we live in; working to make a difference, to achieve something of value—and, for many of us, seeking and finding nourishment in a deeper spiritual connection to life.

Becoming Engaged with Life: A Healing Journey

As I've worked to transform my own patterns of overspending, it's become clearer and clearer to me that when I'm deeply in touch with my inner feelings, I feel less of an urge to shop and acquire things to fill myself up.

Last fall, for example, I noticed a sharp decline in my usual overspending habits. Fall is the season of my birthday and the birthdays of many relatives and friends, and I often find myself buying small and large gifts for myself as I go about shopping for others. It's always been an intense time, a mixture of celebrations and mourning as I remember the loved ones who passed away during this season of the year.

This time, I immersed myself in my own grieving process as I prepared a memorial service filled with songs in honor of my closest childhood friend, who had just died of AIDS. As I began collecting the songs he'd loved, singing them to myself and playing them for others, and remembering him as fully as I could, I noticed with amazement that I was "filling myself up" with these songs, with my own appreciation for Tom and his extraordinary qualities, and with sorrow at his death. Almost miraculously, it seemed, the compulsion to shop—to buy myself the comfort and gratification I usually needed at this time of year—was gone.

Though I'd been teaching clients for years about the importance of seeking out and fulfilling their real, deeper needs instead of settling for the surface self-indulgence which overspending represents, this was the most powerful experience I'd had of the truth of my own words. When shopaholics fill themselves up with their own feelings, intuitions, insights, and healthy actions, they obliterate—at least for a time—the need to fill themselves up by spending money and buying things. It may sound paradoxical to feel filled up with a sense of loss, but that was exactly what happened during this rich and healing fall season.

Will I ever be able to say I'm a recovered spender instead of a recovering one? I doubt I'll ever become a happy hoarder, to whom self-denial is easy and saving money comes naturally. Although music and singing have become a cornerstone of my healing, I'll probably always have to fight periods of stress when that tidal-wave urge to shop sweeps over me. I may even have to keep struggling against the inner tantrums I want to throw when I feel deprived.

But I'm no longer the helplessly driven spender that I was. I've been able to save money to help finance important family purchases and activities, postponing immediate pleasure in order to enjoy greater fulfillment. This growth experience has been enormously valuable, both emotionally and spiritually, in deepening my sense of maturity and groundedness.

> ## Track Your Progress Over Time

I have one last quiz for you both,[1] designed to reflect the progress you've made in *Overcoming Overspending*. After marking down your answers now, I suggest you take this quiz again six months or a year from today . . . because when you finish this book, your progress will be just beginning.

	Now	6 Months from Now	A Year from Now
We understand our attitudes toward money and are working to "move toward the middle" together.	yes/no	yes/no	yes/no
We communicate frequently, openly, and respectfully with each other about our money situation and our feelings about it.	yes/no	yes/no	yes/no
We have a spending plan that is working well for us.	yes/no	yes/no	yes/no
Excluding our home mortgage, we pay off all our debt every month.	yes/no	yes/no	yes/no
We have a reserve fund of two to six months' living expenses.	yes/no	yes/no	yes/no
We save at least 10 percent of every paycheck.	yes/no	yes/no	yes/no
We seldom shop without a list.	yes/no	yes/no	yes/no
We routinely comparison-shop or read consumer product reviews before making major purchases.	yes/no	yes/no	yes/no

	Now	6 Months from Now	A Year from Now
We haven't deliberately made a late payment in at least six months.	yes/no	yes/no	yes/no
We are comfortable with our money and don't feel controlled by it.	yes/no	yes/no	yes/no

Early in this book I expressed hope that as we near the threshold of a new century, we would see the dawning of a more balanced consciousness in our spendaholic culture. A new era when we would achieve the golden balance between consuming and producing—

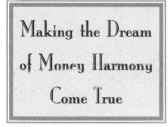

Making the Dream of Money Harmony Come True

buying only what we need to live fully and using our creativity and talents to give back more value than we take. As healers, teachers, builders, leaders, we would share these "gifts" in outward-rippling rings of community and connectedness. Completely at ease with money, we would attain exactly the right balance of giving and receiving, of spending and saving within ourselves and in our relationships.

This is the dream of money harmony . . . an American Dream of the twenty-first century. To make it happen, you needn't give away all your possessions—you just need to face your fear of loneliness and transform your lopsided habits born of old emotional baggage.

I wish you success in overcoming overspending and hope my experience as a therapist and a recovering overspender helps you restore balance in your moneylife.

The lessons I've learned on this journey are my gift to you.

Notes

1. BORN TO SHOP

Many of the statistics in this chapter are quoted by the New Road Map Foundation in *All-Consuming Passion: Waking Up from the American Dream*, second edition (Seattle, 1993). Where possible, I've referenced the original sources for these statistics.

1. For more information on our society's changing attitudes toward money, see Warren I. Susman, *Culture as History: The Transformation of American Society in the Twentieth Century* (New York: Pantheon Books, 1984), pp. xx–xxix.
2. Victor Lebow, *Journal of Retailing* (publication date unknown), quoted in *The Waste Makers* by Vance Packard (New York: David McKay, 1960).
3. Alan Thein Durning, *How Much Is Enough? The Consumer Society and the Future of the Earth* (New York: W. W. Norton & Co., Inc., 1992), p. 128.

4. Betsy Morris, "Big Spenders: As a Favored Pastime, Shopping Ranks High with Most Americans," *The Wall Street Journal*, July 30, 1987.

5. Laurence Shames, *The Hunger for More* (New York: Times Books, 1989), p. 147.

6. Sam Keen, Lecture: "Your Mythic Journey: Finding Meaning in Your Life," Common Boundary Conference on Sacred Stories, Crystal City. Va. November 13, 1991.

7. Morris, *op. cit.*

8. Lillian Africano, "Born-Again Consumers," *On the Issues*, Summer 1994, pp. 32–34.

9. Robert Eisner, "We Don't Need Balanced Budgets," *The Wall Street Journal*, January 11, 1995. Eisner's figure of $4.5 trillion in current U.S. household debt is one-third higher than the 1990 figure of $3.4 trillion reported by Lani Luciano in "How to Cut Your Expenses 20% (and Live Better Too)," *Money*, December 1991, pp. 70–75.

10. Luciano, *op. cit.*, p. 70.

11. Mary Granfield, "Having It All in America Today," *Money*, October 1991, p. 124.

12. "Record Number Going Broke," *Seattle Times*, September 5, 1991.

13. Source for 1973 figure: Charles Wold, Jr., "Our Problem Isn't So Much Borrowing," *The Wall Street Journal*, September 28, 1984. Source for 1993 figure: Fred R. Bleakley, "The Outlook: Taxes Will Go Higher; So Will Spending Fall?", *The Wall Street Journal*, December 6, 1993.

14. David Wallechinsky and Irving Wallace, *The People's Almanac* (Garden City, N.Y.: Doubleday & Co., 1975), p. 341.

15. American Bankers Association, quoted by Peter Keating, "How to Avoid Being Swamped By Your Credit-Card Debt," *Money*, March 1995, p. 40.

16. *Ibid.*

17. Ruth Susswein, executive director of Bankcard Holders of America, Phone conversation, March 10, 1995.

18. National Foundation for Consumer Credit statistics provided by CCCS of Maine, Inc.

19. The National Foundation for Consumer Credit; and John H. Cushman, Jr., "Bankrupt Individuals Are Fewer," *New York Times*, June 28, 1993.
20. Alan L. Otten, "Young Adults Now Are More Pessimistic," *The Wall Street Journal*, September 27, 1993.
21. John Cunniff, "Would You Believe These Are the Good Old Days?" *Seattle Times*, September 19, 1993.

2. WHY DO WE OVERSPEND?

1. For more information on spenders, hoarders, bingers, and other money types, see my first book, *Money Harmony: Resolving Money Conflicts in Your Life and Relationships* (New York: Walker and Company, 1994).
2. Among other sources for this: Gloria Arenson, *Born to Spend: How to Overcome Compulsive Spending* (Bradenton, Fla.: TAB Books, 1992), pp. 1–4; and Susan Forward, *Money Demons: Keep Them from Sabotaging Your Relationships—and Your Life* (New York: Bantam Books, 1994), p. 105.
3. These profiles are inspired by a similar breakdown by J. Grady Cash, C.F.P., and Kathy K. Cash, R.N., in *Conquer the 7 Deadly Money Mistakes: The No Math, No-Hassle, Values-Based Way to Reach Your Financial Dreams* (Hampton, Va.: Center for Financial Well-Being, 1994), p. 5. I've made some modifications in Cash's categories to reflect my personal and clinical experience.

3. "IT SWEEPS OVER ME LIKE A TIDAL WAVE"

1. This explanation is closely patterned on the six phases Gloria Arenson outlines in *Born to Spend*, pp. 52–54. I've combined the last two phases she describes into one (the letdown).

4. OVERSPENDERS AND THOSE
WHO LOVE THEM

1. Melody Beattie, *Codependent No More: How to Stop Controlling Others and Start Caring for Yourself* (New York: Harper/Hazelden, 1987).

6. BREAKING THE BONDS OF
SECRECY AND SHAME

1. As I mention earlier in this book, I prefer not to take a stand on whether or not overspending is an actual physical addiction. However, here and elsewhere in *Overcoming Overspending*, I'll use "addiction" in its colloquial sense of a hard-to-resist urge or powerful compulsion.

7. THE ABCs OF SUPPORTIVE
COMMUNICATION

1. I learned these specific empathetic listening techniques from Isaiah Zimmerman, Ph.D., a Washington-based psychologist who taught me his communications "structure" over twenty years ago, and from Harville Hendrix in a workshop on "Marriage As a Path to Wholeness," Common Boundary Conference on Visible Threads, Washington, D.C., November 13, 1992.

8. WORKING IT OUT TOGETHER

1. You'll find this exercise described in detail on page 260 (paperback edition) of Harville Hendrix's *Getting the Love You Want: A Guide for Couples* (New York: Harper & Row, 1990).

2. This is based on an exercise that Christopher Mogil and Anne Slepian call "Reflecting on Our Daily Lives." For more about it, see their workbook, *Getting Along: Communication Skills to Help You and Your Loved Ones Move Gracefully Together Through Everyday Life* (Arlington, Mass.: The Impact Project, 1992), p. 33.

3. This exercise appears in several of John Gray's books. I found it in his highly popular *Men Are from Mars, Women Are from Venus* (New York: HarperCollins, 1992), p. 209.

10. FIGHTING OFF TEMPTATION

1. You can find more about this technique in Susan Forward's *Money Demons* (New York: Bantam Books, 1994), p. 113.

2. I've borrowed the "changing the tape" example Gloria Arenson describes more fully in *Born to Spend* (Bradenton, Fla.: TAB Books, 1992), p. 70.

3. Some of these assignments are my own; others are adapted from J. Grady Cash's *Conquer the 7 Deadly Money Mistakes*, p. 7. See Bibliography for ordering this self-published workbook.

4. Some of these suggestions were inspired by Vicki Robin's article "Purging the Urge to Splurge: 50 Simple Things You Can Do Instead of Shopping," *In Context*, Summer 1990, pp. 36–39.

5. This information about DA comes from a series of informational pamphlets given out to DA members.

6. This information about CCCS and its clients was provided by CCCS of Maine, one of its statewide affiliates.

11. FIVE WHO OVERCAME

1. You can find more information about this technique in Pat McCallum's *Stepping Free of Limiting Patterns with Essence Repatterning*™ (Washington, D.C.: Source Unlimited, 1992).

JOURNEY'S END

1. This quiz for recovering overspenders and their partners is comprised
    of some of my own questions and some adapted from J. Grady Cash's
    "Empowered Consumer Test" (*Conquer the 7 Deadly Money Mistakes*, p. 37).

Bibliography

Starred entries have special relevance to overcoming overspending. If an older book is no longer in print, you may be able to find it at your local library or through an interlibrary loan.

GENERAL REFERENCE FOR
OVERSPENDERS AND THEIR
PARTNERS

*Arenson, Gloria. *Born to Spend: How to Overcome Compulsive Spending.* Bradenton, Fla.: TAB Books (div. of McGraw-Hill, Inc.), Human Services Institute, 1992.

*Bryan, Mark, and Julia Cameron. *The Money Drunk: 90 Days to Financial Freedom.* New York: Ballantine Books, 1993.

*Cash, J. Grady, C.F.P., and Kathy K. Cash, R.N. *Conquer the 7 Deadly Money Mistakes: The No-Math, No-Hassle, Values-Based Way to Reach*

Your Financial Dreams. Hampton, Va.: Center for Financial Well-Being, 1994. (To order this self-published workbook, call (804) 851-7440 or write the Center for Financial Well-Being, P.O. Box 65695, Hampton, VA 23665-0695.)

*Damon, Janet E. *Shopaholics.* Los Angeles: Price Stern Sloan, 1988.

*Dominguez, Joe, and Vicki Robin. *Your Money or Your Life: Transforming Your Relationship with Money and Achieving Financial Independence.* New York: Viking, 1992.

Felton-Collins, Victoria, with Suzanne Blair Brown. *Couples and Money: Why Money Interferes with Love and What to Do About It.* New York: Bantam Books, 1990.

*Forward, Susan, and Craig Buck. *Money Demons: Keep Them from Sabotaging Your Relationships—and Your Life.* New York: Bantam Books, 1994.

Lieberman, Annette, and Vicky Lindner. *Unbalanced Accounts: How Women Can Overcome Their Fear of Money.* New York: Penguin Books, 1988.

Matthews, Arlene Modica. *Your Money, Your Self: Understanding and Improving Your Relationship to Cash and Credit.* New York: Fireside Books, 1993.

*Mellan, Olivia. *Money Harmony: Resolving Money Conflicts in Your Life and Relationships.* New York: Walker and Company, 1994.

*Mundis, Jerrold. *How to Get Out of Debt, Stay Out of Debt, and Live Prosperously.* New York: Bantam Books, 1990.

Schmookler, Andrew Bard. *Fool's Gold: The Fate of Values in a World of Goods.* New York: HarperCollins, 1993.

Sinetar, Marsha. *Do What You Love, the Money Will Follow: Discovering Your Right Livelihood.* New York: Paulist Press, 1987.

Waldman, Mark. *The Way of Real Wealth.* New York: HarperCollins, 1993.

Weinstein, Grace. *Men, Women & Money: New Roles, New Rules.* New York: New American Library, 1986.

*Wesson, Carolyn. *Women Who Shop Too Much: Overcoming the Urge to Splurge.* New York: St. Martin's Press, 1990.

BOOKS ABOUT COUPLE
RELATIONSHIPS AND CONFLICT
RESOLUTION

Farrell, Warren. *The Myth of Male Power.* New York: Simon & Schuster, 1993.

Farrell, Warren. *Why Men Are the Way They Are: The Male-Female Dynamic.* New York: McGraw-Hill, 1986.

Fisher, Roger, and William Ury. *Getting to Yes: Negotiating Agreement Without Giving In.* New York: Penguin Books, 1983.

Gray, John. *Men Are from Mars, Women Are from Venus.* New York: HarperCollins, 1992.

———. *What Your Mother Couldn't Tell You and Your Father Didn't Know.* New York: HarperCollins, 1994.

Hendrix, Harville. *Getting the Love You Want: A Guide for Couples.* New York: Harper & Row, 1990.

———. *Keeping the Love You Find: A Personal Guide.* New York: Pocket Books/Simon & Schuster, 1992.

Louden, Jennifer. *The Couple's Comfort Book: A Creative Guide for Renewing Passion, Pleasure and Commitment.* HarperSanFrancisco, 1994.

Mogil, Christopher, and Anne Slepian. *Getting Along: Communication Skills to Help You and Your Loved Ones Move Gracefully Together Through Everyday Life.* Arlington. Mass.: The Impact Project, 1992. (To order this self-published book, call (617) 648-0776 or write The Impact Project, 21 Linwood Street, Arlington, MA 02174.)

Rubin, Lillian. *Intimate Strangers: Men and Women Together.* New York: Harper & Row, 1983.

Woodhouse, Violet, and Victoria Felton-Collins, with M. C. Blakeman. *Divorce & Money: Everything You Need to Know About Dividing Property.* Nolo Press, Self-Help Law, 1992.

BOOKS ABOUT PSYCHOLOGY,
SOCIOLOGY, AND CHANGE

*Beattie, Melody. *Codependent No More: How to Stop Controlling Others and Start Caring for Yourself.* New York: Harper/Hazelden, 1987.
*Cameron, Julia, with Mark Bryan. *The Artist's Way: A Spiritual Path to Higher Creativity.* New York: Jeremy Tarcher/Putnam (G.P. Putnam's Sons), 1992.
Lerner, Harriet Goldhor. *The Dance of Intimacy.* New York: Harper & Row, 1991.
————. *The Dance of Anger: A Woman's Guide to Changing the Patterns of Intimate Relationships.* New York: Harper & Row, 1985.
————. *The Dance of Deception: Pretending and Truth-telling in Women's Lives.* New York: HarperCollins, 1994.
McCallum, Pat. *Stepping Free of Limiting Patterns with Essence Repatterning*™. Washington, D.C.: Source Unlimited, 1992. (To order this book or any of her audiocassettes, which teach you how to do this process by yourself, write to Source Unlimited, P.O. Box 15826, Chevy Chase, Md. 20815.)
*Susman, Warren I. *Culture as History: The Transformation of American Society in the Twentieth Century.* New York: Pantheon Books, 1984.

BOOKS ABOUT PERSONAL
FINANCE

Claflin, Edward, and Sid Kitchheimer, eds. *Cut Your Spending In Half without Settling for Less.* Emmaus, Penn.: Rodale Press, 1994.
Cotton, Kathleen L. *Financial Planning for the Not Yet Wealthy.* Redmond, Wash.: FinPlan Publishing, 1987.
*Dacyczyn, Amy. *The Tightwad Gazette: Promoting Thrift as a Viable Alternative Lifestyle.* New York: Villard Books, 1993.
Quinn, Jane Bryant. *Making the Most of Your Money: Smart Ways to*

Create Wealth and Plan Your Finances in the '90s. New York: Simon & Schuster, 1991.

ARTICLES, PAMPHLETS AND
NEWSLETTERS

Barber, Judy. *Family Money* (quarterly newsletter), 1515 Fourth St., Suite B, Napa, CA 94559 (707) 255-6254.

Hom, Tony, M.B.A., J.D., with Edward Claflin. *Master Your Money Power* (excerpted from *Smart, Successful, and Broke: the 6-Step Action Plan for Getting Out of Debt and Into the Money*). Emmaus, Penn.: Rodale Press, 1994.

ᴬRobin, Vicki. "Purging the Urge to Splurge: 50 Simple Things You Can Do Instead of Shopping." *In Context*, No. 26 (Summer 1990), pp. 36–39. (This quarterly is published by Context Institute, P.O. Box 11470, Bainbridge Island, WA 98110.)

The Impact Project's Newsletter. *More than Money*. 2244 Alder Street, Eugene, OR 97405. (503) 343-2420.

ᴬThe New Road Map Foundation. *All-Consuming Passion: Waking Up from the American Dream* (second edition). Seattle, Wash., 1993. (For more information, write The New Road Map Foundation at P.O. Box 15981, Seattle, WA 98115.)

MATERIALS TO HELP TEACH
CHILDREN SENSIBLE MONEY
HABITS

Bodnar, Janet. *Kiplinger's Money-Smart Kids (And Parents Too!)*. Washington, D.C.: Kiplinger Books, 1995.

Lewin, Elizabeth, C.F.P., and Bernard Ryan, Jr. *Simple Ways to Help Your Kids Become Dollar Smart*. New York: Walker and Company, 1994.

*Beware of the Credit Monster: Win the War for Your Dollars: A Guide for
   Young Adults* (audiocassette tapes). Write Venture Forward, Inc., P.O.
   Box 62158, St. Louis Park, MN 55426; or call (612) 938-7042.

OTHER RESOURCES

Consumer Credit Counseling Services will provide information on setting up a spending plan, and will help in cases of serious indebtedness by structuring a Debt Management Plan which you and your
   creditors agree to follow. To find the CCCS office nearest you, call
   (800) 388-2227.

Debtors Anonymous will provide support and help in developing an action plan to change your spending patterns and reduce debt. To find
   the nearest DA group, call (212) 642-8220.

Gamblers Anonymous is an organization that helps people identify, prevent, and treat compulsive gambling. To speak with a volunteer or obtain more information, call (800) GAMBLER (426-2537).

The National Institute for Consumer Education (NICE) acts as a clearing-
   house for information to help you manage your money better, including
   lists of free publications. For more information, call (800) 336-6423 or
   write The National Institute for Consumer Education, 207 Rackham
   Building, Eastern Michigan University, Ypsilanti, MI 48197.

Index